新丝路"中文＋职业技能"系列教材编写委员会
（中文＋汽车服务）

总策划：马箭飞　谢永华

策　划：邵旭波　邵亦鹏　张海宁

顾　问：朱志平（北京师范大学）
　　　　林秀琴（首都师范大学）
　　　　宋继华（北京师范大学）

总主编：谢永华　杜曾慧

语言类主编：易　华

语言类副主编：周　波　史其慧

专业类副主编：丁继斌　邱亚宇　王秀梅　杨康

项目组长：郭凤岚

项目副组长：付彦白

项目成员：郭　冰　武传霞　齐　琰　赫　栗　李金梅　张　彪

新丝路"中文+职业技能"系列教材
New Silk Road "Chinese + Vocational Skills" Series

中文+汽车服务工程技术

Chinese + Automotive Service Engineering Technology

中级 Intermediate

新丝路"中文+职业技能"系列教材编写委员会 编

北京语言大学出版社
BEIJING LANGUAGE AND CULTURE UNIVERSITY PRESS

© 2024 北京语言大学出版社，社图号 23246

图书在版编目（CIP）数据

中文＋汽车服务工程技术．中级／新丝路"中文＋职业技能"系列教材编写委员会编．－－北京：北京语言大学出版社，2024.4

新丝路"中文＋职业技能"系列教材

ISBN 978-7-5619-6461-3

Ⅰ.①中… Ⅱ.①新… Ⅲ.①汉语－对外汉语教学－教材②汽车工业－销售管理－商业服务－教材 Ⅳ.① H195.4 ② F407.471.5

中国国家版本馆 CIP 数据核字（2024）第 021770 号

中文＋汽车服务工程技术（中级）
ZHONGWEN + QICHE FUWU GONGCHENG JISHU (ZHONGJI)

排版制作：	北京创艺涵文化发展有限公司
责任印制：	周 燚

出版发行：	北京语言大学出版社
社　　址：	北京市海淀区学院路 15 号，100083
网　　址：	www.blcup.com
电子信箱：	service@blcup.com
电　　话：	编 辑 部 8610-82303647/3592/3724
	国内发行 8610-82303650/3591/3648
	海外发行 8610-82303365/3080/3668
	北语书店 8610-82303653
	网购咨询 8610-82303908
印　　刷：	北京富资园科技发展有限公司

版　次：	2024 年 4 月第 1 版	印　次：	2024 年 4 月第 1 次印刷
开　本：	889 毫米 × 1194 毫米 1/16	印　张：	10.75
字　数：	173 千字		
定　价：	98.00 元		

PRINTED IN CHINA

凡有印装质量问题，本社负责调换。售后 QQ 号 1367565611，电话 010-82303590

编写说明

新丝路"中文+职业技能"系列教材是把中文作为第二语言,结合专业和职业的专门用途、职业用途的中文教材,不是专业理论教材,不是一般意义的通用综合中文教材。本系列教材定位为职场生存中文教材、立体式技能型语言教材。教材研发的目标是既要满足学习者一般中文环境下的基本交际需求,又要满足学习者职业学习需求和职场工作需求。它和普通的国际中文教材的区别不在语法,而在词汇的专门化程度,在中文的用途、使用场合、应用范围。目前,专门用途、职业用途的中文教材在语言分类和研究成果上几近空白,本系列教材的成功研发开创了中文学习的新视野、新领域、新方向,将"中文+职业技能+X等级证书"真正融合,使学习者在学习中文的同时,也可通过实践掌握职业技能,从而获得 X 等级证书。

适用对象

本系列教材将适用对象定位为双零基础(零语言基础、零技能基础)的来华学习中文和先进技能的长期或者短期进修生,可满足初、中、高各层次专业课程的教学需要。教材亦可供海内外相关的培训课程及"走出去"的中资企业培训本土化员工使用。

结构规模

本系列教材采取专项语言技能与职业技能训练相结合的中文教学及教材编写模式。教材选择当前热门的物流管理、汽车服务工程技术、电子商务、机电一体化、计算机网络技术、酒店管理等六个专业,培养各专业急需急用的技术岗位人才。每个专业教材均包括初、中、高级三册。每一册都配有专业视频教学资源,还附有"视频脚本""参考答案"等配套资源。

编写理念

本系列教材将词语进行分类,区分普通词语和专业词语,以通用语料为基础,以概念性、行为性词语为主,不脱离职场情境讨论分级,做到控制词汇量,控制工作场景,控制交流内容与方式,构建语义框架。将语言的分级和专业的分级科学地融合,是实现本系列教材成功编写的关键。

教材目标

语言技能目标:

初级阶段,能熟练掌握基础通用词语和职场的常用专业词语,能使用简短句子进行简单的生活及工作交流。中级阶段，能听懂工作场合简单的交谈与发言，明白大意，把握基本情况，能就工作中重要的话题用简单的话与人沟通。高级阶段，能听懂工作场合一般的交谈与发言，抓住主要内容和关键信息，使用基本交际策略与人交流、开展工作，能初步了解与交际活动相关的文化因素，掌握与交际有关的一般文化背景知识，能排除交际时遇到的文化障碍。交际能力层次的递进实现从初级的常规礼节、基本生活及工作的交流能力，到中级的简单的服务流程信息交流能力，最后达到高级的复杂信息的交流和特情处理的能力。

职业技能目标：

以满足岗位需求为目标，将遴选出的当前热门的专业工作岗位分为初、中、高三级。物流管理专业初、中、高级对应的岗位分别是物流员、物流经理、物流总监；汽车服务工程技术专业初、中、高级对应的岗位分别是汽车机电维修工、汽车服务顾问、技术总监；电子商务专业初、中、高级对应的岗位分别是电子商务运营助理、电子商务运营员、电子商务客服；机电一体化专业初、中、高级对应的岗位分别是机电操作工、机电调整工、机电维修工；计算机网络技术专业初、中、高级对应的岗位分别是宽带运维工程师、网络运维专员、网络管理员；酒店管理专业初、中、高级对应的岗位分别是前厅基层接待员、前厅主管、前厅经理。每个专业分解出三十个工作场景/任务，学习者在学习后能够全面掌握此岗位的概况及基本程序，实现语言学习和专业操作的双重目标。

编写原则

1. 语言知识技能与专业知识技能并进，满足当前热门的、急需急用的岗位需求。

2. 渐进分化，综合贯通，拆解难点，分而治之。

3. 语言知识与专业知识科学、高效复现，语言技能与专业技能螺旋式上升，职场情境、语义框架、本体输入方式相互配合。

4. 使用大量的图片和视频，实现专业知识和技能呈现形式可视化。

5. 强化专业岗位实操性技能。本系列教材配有专业技术教学的视频，突出展示专业岗位的实操性技能，语言学习难度与技能掌握难度的不匹配可通过实操性强的视频和实训环节来补充。

特色追求

本系列教材从初级最基础的语音知识学习和岗位认知开始，将"中文＋职业技能"融入在工作场景对话中，把工作分解成一个个任务，用图片认知的方式解决专业词语的认知问题，用视频展示的方法解决学习者掌握中文词语与专业技能的不匹配问题，注重技能的实操性，注重"在做中学"。每一单元都设置了"学以致用"板块，目的不仅仅是解决本单元任务的词语认知问题，更是将学习的目标放在"能听""能用""能模仿说出"上。我们力争通过大量图片的使用和配套视频的展示，将教材打造成立体式、技能型语言教材，方便学习者能够更好地自主学习。

使用建议

1. 本系列教材每个专业分为初、中、高级三册，每册10单元，初级每单元建议8～10课时完成，中级10～12课时完成，高级12～14课时完成。

2. 教材注释和说明着力于简明扼要，注重实操性，注重听说技能培养，对于教材涉及的语法知识，教师可视情况予以细化和补充。

3. "单元实训"板块可以在课文和语言点学完之后作为课堂练习使用，建议2课时完成。教师要带着学习者按照实训步骤一步步完成，实训步骤不要求学习者能够看懂，读懂，重要的是教师要引领操作，实现学习者掌握专业技能的目标。

4. "单元小结"板块是对整个单元关键词语和核心内容的总结，对于这部分内容，教师要进行听说练习，以便更好地帮助学习者了解本单元的核心工作任务。

5. 教师上课时要充分利用教材设计的练习，引导学习者多听多练，听说结合，学做合一。

6. 教师要带着学习者熟练诵读课文，要求学习者把每课的关键词语和句子、课堂用语背诵下来。

特别感谢

感谢教育部中外语言交流合作中心将新丝路"中文＋职业技能"系列教材列为重点研发项目，为我们教材编写增添了动力和责任感。教材编写委员会负责整套教材的规划、设计与编写协调，并先后召开上百次讨论会，对每册教材的课文编写、体例安排、注释说明、练习设计、图片选择、视频制作等进行全方位的评估、讨论和审定。感谢编写委员会成员和所有编者高度的敬业精神、精益求精的编写态度，以及所投入的热情和精力、付出的心血与智慧。感谢关注本系列教材并贡献宝贵意见的国际中文教育教学界专家和全国各地的同人。

新丝路"中文＋职业技能"系列教材编写委员会
2023年4月

Compilation Instructions

The New Silk Road "Chinese + Vocational Skills" is a series of Chinese textbooks for specialized and vocational purposes that combine professional and vocational technologies with Chinese as a second language. Instead of being specialized theoretical textbooks, or comprehensive or universal Chinese textbooks in a general sense, this series is intended to be Chinese textbooks for career survival, and three-dimensional skills-based language textbooks. The textbooks are developed with a view to meeting students' basic communication needs in general Chinese environment, and their professional learning needs and workplace demands as well. They are different from ordinary Chinese textbooks for foreigners in the degree of specialization of vocabulary, in the purpose, usage occasion, and application scope of Chinese (not in grammar). At present, Chinese textbooks for specialized and vocational purposes are virtually non-existent in terms of language classification and research results, so the successful development of this series has opened up new horizons, new fields and new directions for Chinese learning, and virtually integrated "Chinese + Vocational Skills + X-Level Certificates", which enables students to practically master vocational skills and obtain X-level certificates while learning Chinese.

Applicable Targets

This series is targeted at long-term or short-term students who come to China to learn Chinese and advanced skills with zero language basis and zero skill basis, which can meet the teaching needs of the elementary, intermediate and advanced specialized courses. This series can also be used for relevant training courses at home and abroad and for Chinese-funded enterprises that "go global" to train local employees.

Structure and Scale

This series adopts a Chinese teaching and textbook compilation model combining special language skills and vocational skills training. The series includes the textbooks for six popular majors such as logistics management, automotive service engineering technology, e-commerce, mechatronics, computer networking technology, and hotel management to cultivate technical talents in urgent need. The textbooks for each major consist of the textbooks at the elementary, intermediate and advanced levels. Each textbook is equipped with professional video teaching resources, and "video scripts", "reference answers" and other supporting resources as well.

Compilation Concept

This series classifies the vocabulary into general vocabulary and specialized vocabulary. Based on the general vocabulary, it focuses on conceptual and behavioral words, not deviating from workplace situations, so as to control the vocabulary, work scenarios and content and means of communication, and build the semantic framework. The scientific integration of language classification and specialty classification is the key to the successful compilation of textbooks.

Textbook Objectives

Language Skill Objectives

For students at the elementary level, they are trained to be familiar with basic general vocabulary and common specialized vocabulary in the workplace, and be able to use short sentences for simple communication in life and at work. For those at the intermediate level, they are trained to understand simple conversations and speeches in the workplace, comprehend the main ideas, grasp the basic situations, and communicate with others in simple words on important topics at work. For those at the advanced level, they are trained to be able to understand general conversations and speeches in the workplace, grasp the main content and key information, use basic communication strategies to communicate with others and carry out the work, have a preliminary understanding of cultural factors related to communication activities, master the general communication-related cultural background knowledge, and overcome cultural barriers encountered during communication. The progression in level of communicative competence helps them to leap forward from routine etiquette, basic communication in life and at work at the elementary level, to simple information exchange of service processes at the intermediate level, and finally to complex information exchange and handling of special circumstances at the advanced level.

Vocational Skill Objectives

To meet job requirements at the elementary, intermediate and advanced levels, the professional positions that are most urgently needed overseas are selected. The positions corresponding to logistics management at the elementary, intermediate and advanced levels are logistics staff, logistics managers and logistics directors; the positions corresponding to automotive service engineering technology at the elementary, intermediate and advanced levels are automotive electromechanical maintenance staff, automotive service consultants and technical directors; the positions corresponding to e-commerce at the elementary, intermediate and advanced levels are electronic operation assistants, e-commerce operators and e-commerce customer service staff; the positions corresponding to mechatronics at the elementary, intermediate and advanced levels are mechanical and electrical operators, mechanical and electrical adjusters, and mechanical and electrical maintenance staff; the positions corresponding to computer networking technology at the elementary, intermediate and advanced levels are broadband operation and maintenance engineers, network operation and maintenance specialists, and network administrators; the positions corresponding to hotel management at the elementary, intermediate and advanced levels are lobby receptionists, lobby supervisors and lobby managers. Through 30 work scenarios/tasks set for each major, learners can fully grasp the general situations and basic procedures of the position after learning, and achieve the dual goals of language learning and professional operation.

Principles of Compilation

1. Language knowledge skills and professional knowledge skills go hand in hand to meet the demands of current popular and urgently needed job positions;

2. It makes progressive differentiation and comprehensive integration, breaking down, dividing and conquering difficult points;

3. Language knowledge and professional knowledge recur scientifically and efficiently, language skills and professional skills spiral upward, and the situational stage, semantic framework, and ontology input methods cooperate with each other;

4. Professional knowledge and skills are visualized, using a lot of pictures and videos;

5. It strengthens the practical skills in professional positions. This series of textbooks is equipped with videos of professional technical training, highlighting the practical skills for professional positions. It addresses the mismatch between the difficulty of language learning and that of mastering skills by supplementing with practical videos and practical training.

Characteristic Pursuit

Starting from the basic phonetic knowledge learning and job cognition at the elementary level, this series integrates "Chinese + Vocational Skills" into the working scene dialogues, breaking down the job into various tasks, solving lexical students' problems by means of picture cognition, solving the problem of the mismatch between students' mastery of Chinese vocabulary and professional skills by means of displaying videos, stressing the practicality of skills, and focusing on "learning by doing". Each unit has a "Practicing What You Have Learnt" module, which not only solves the problem of lexical cognition of this unit, but also takes "being able to comprehend", "being able to use" and "being able to imitate" as the learning objectives. We strive to use a large number of pictures and display supporting videos to build the textbooks into three-dimensional skills-based language teaching materials, so that learners can learn more independently.

Recommendations for Use

1. Each major of this series consists of three volumes at the elementary, intermediate, and advanced levels, with 10 units in each volume. For each unit, it is recommended to be completed in 8-10 class hours at the elementary level, 10-12 class hours at the intermediate level, and 12-14 class hours at the advanced level.

2. The notes and explanations in the textbooks focus on conciseness, practicality, and the training of listening and speaking skills. The grammar knowledge in the textbooks can be detailed and supplemented by teachers as the case may be.

3. "Unit Practical Training" module can be used as a classroom exercise after the texts and language points, preferably to be completed in two class hours. Teachers should guide students to complete the training tasks step by step. Students are not required to read and understand the training steps. It is important that teachers guide students to achieve the goal of mastering professional skills.

4. "Unit Summary" module summarizes the keywords and core content of the entire unit. Through listening and speaking exercises, this part can better help learners understand the core tasks of this unit.

5. Teachers should make full use of the exercises designed in the textbooks during class, and guide students to listen more and practice more, combine listening and speaking, and integrate learning with practice.

6. Teachers should guide students to proficiently read the texts aloud, asking them to recite the keywords, sentences and classroom expressions in each unit.

Acknowledgements

We are grateful to the Center for Language Education and Cooperation of the Ministry of Education for listing the New Silk Road "Chinese + Vocational Skills" series as a key research and development project, which adds motivation and a sense of responsibility to our textbook compilation. The Textbook Compilation Committee is responsible for the planning, design, compilation and coordination of the entire set of textbooks, and has held hundreds of seminars to conduct a comprehensive evaluation, discussion, examination and approval of text compilation, style arrangement, notes and explanations, exercise design, picture selection, and video production of each textbook. We are indebted to the members of the Compilation Committee and all compilers for their professional dedication, unwavering pursuit of perfection in the compilation, as well as their enthusiasm, hard work and wisdom. We are thankful to the experts in international Chinese language education and colleagues from all over the country who have kept a close eye on this series and contributed their valuable opinions.

Compilation Committee of New Silk Road "Chinese + Vocational Skills" Series

April 2023

rénwù jièshào
人物介绍
Introduction to Characters

shīfu
师傅
Master

xuétú　túdi
学徒（徒弟）
Apprentice

jīdiàn wéixiūgōng
机电维修工
Mechanical and Electrical Maintenance Technician

jìshù zǒngjiān
技术总监
Technical Director

fúwù gùwèn
服务顾问
Service Consultant

kèhù
客户
Customer

语法术语及缩略形式参照表
Abbreviations of Grammar Terms

Grammar Terms in Chinese	Grammar Terms in Pinyin	Grammar Terms in English	Abbreviations
名词	míngcí	noun	n.
专有名词	zhuānyǒu míngcí	proper noun	pn.
代词	dàicí	pronoun	pron.
数词	shùcí	numeral	num.
量词	liàngcí	measure word	m.
数量词	shùliàngcí	quantifier	q.
动词	dòngcí	verb	v.
助动词	zhùdòngcí	auxiliary	aux.
形容词	xíngróngcí	adjective	adj.
副词	fùcí	adverb	adv.
介词	jiècí	preposition	prep.
连词	liáncí	conjunction	conj.
助词	zhùcí	particle	part.
拟声词	nǐshēngcí	onomatopoeia	onom.
叹词	tàncí	interjection	int.
前缀	qiánzhuì	prefix	pref.
后缀	hòuzhuì	suffix	suf.
成语	chéngyǔ	idiom	idm.
短语	duǎnyǔ	phrase	phr.
主语	zhǔyǔ	subject	S
谓语	wèiyǔ	predicate	P
宾语	bīnyǔ	object	O
定语	dìngyǔ	attributive	Attrib
状语	zhuàngyǔ	adverbial	Adverb
补语	bǔyǔ	complement	C

CONTENTS 目录

第一单元　电动汽车简介　Unit 1　Introduction to Electric Vehicles　1

- 第一部分　课文　**Texts**　2
  - 一、热身 Warm-up　2
  - 二、课文 Texts　4
  - 三、视听说 Viewing, Listening and Speaking　7
  - 四、学以致用 Practicing What You Have Learnt　8
  - 五、小知识 Tips　9
- 第二部分　汉字　**Chinese Characters**　10
  - 一、汉字知识 Knowledge about Chinese Characters　10
    1. 汉字的笔画（1）　Strokes of Chinese characters (1)
       一　丨　丿　丶
    2. 汉字的笔顺（1）　Stroke orders of Chinese characters (1)
       先横后竖 Horizontal strokes before vertical strokes
       先撇后捺 Left-falling strokes before right-falling strokes
  - 二、汉字认读与书写 The Recognition and Writing of Chinese Characters　10
- 第三部分　日常用语　**Daily Expressions**　11
- 第四部分　单元实训　**Unit Practical Training**　11
  - 动力电池充电故障排除 Power Battery Charging Troubleshooting　11
- 第五部分　单元小结　**Unit Summary**　12

第二单元　电动汽车高压电控总成　Unit 2　High-voltage Electronic Control Assembly of Electric Vehicles　15

- 第一部分　课文　**Texts**　16
  - 一、热身 Warm-up　16
  - 二、课文 Texts　18
  - 三、视听说 Viewing, Listening and Speaking　20
  - 四、学以致用 Practicing What You Have Learnt　21
  - 五、小知识 Tips　22

I

第二部分	汉字	**Chinese Characters**	23
	一、汉字知识 Knowledge about Chinese Characters		23

        1. 汉字的笔画（2） Strokes of Chinese characters (2)

          丶 ㇆ ㇄ ㇙

        2. 汉字的笔顺（2） Stroke orders of Chinese characters (2)

        先上后下 Upper strokes before lower strokes

        先左后右 Left-side strokes before right-side strokes

	二、汉字认读与书写 The Recognition and Writing of Chinese Characters		24
第三部分	日常用语	**Daily Expressions**	24
第四部分	单元实训	**Unit Practical Training**	24
	电动汽车高压电控总成 High-voltage Electronic Control Assembly of Electric Vehicles		24
第五部分	单元小结	**Unit Summary**	25

第三单元　电动汽车绝缘检测　Unit 3　Insulation Testing of Electric Vehicles　27

第一部分	课文	**Texts**	28
	一、热身 Warm-up		28
	二、课文 Texts		30
	三、视听说 Viewing, Listening and Speaking		32
	四、学以致用 Practicing What You Have Learnt		33
	五、小知识 Tips		34
第二部分	汉字	**Chinese Characters**	35
	一、汉字知识 Knowledge about Chinese Characters		35

        1. 汉字的笔画（3） Strokes of Chinese characters (3)

          ㇇ 亅 丿 乚

        2. 汉字的笔顺（3） Stroke orders of Chinese characters (3)

        先中间后两边 Strokes in the middle before those on both sides

        先外边后里边 Outside strokes before inside strokes

	二、汉字认读与书写 The Recognition and Writing of Chinese Characters		36
第三部分	日常用语	**Daily Expressions**	36
第四部分	单元实训	**Unit Practical Training**	36
	电动汽车绝缘检测 Insulation Testing of Electric Vehicles		36
第五部分	单元小结	**Unit Summary**	37

第四单元　空调系统　Unit 4　Air Conditioning System　39

第一部分	课文	**Texts**	40
	一、热身 Warm-up		40

二、课文 Texts		42
三、视听说 Viewing, Listening and Speaking		45
四、学以致用 Practicing What You Have Learnt		46
五、小知识 Tips		46
第二部分 汉字 **Chinese Characters**		47
一、汉字知识 Knowledge about Chinese Characters		47
1. 汉字的笔画（4） Strokes of Chinese characters (4)		
㇏ ㇀ ㇁ ㇂		
2. 汉字的笔顺（4） Stroke orders of Chinese characters (4)		
先外后里再封口 Outside strokes before inside strokes, and then sealing strokes		
二、汉字认读与书写 The Recognition and Writing of Chinese Characters		48
第三部分 日常用语 **Daily Expressions**		48
第四部分 单元实训 **Unit Practical Training**		48
正确使用空调系统 Proper Use of Air Conditioning System		48
第五部分 单元小结 **Unit Summary**		49

第五单元　典型传感器　Unit 5　Typical Sensors　51

第一部分 课文 **Texts**		52
一、热身 Warm-up		52
二、课文 Texts		54
三、视听说 Viewing, Listening and Speaking		56
四、学以致用 Practicing What You Have Learnt		57
五、小知识 Tips		58
第二部分 汉字 **Chinese Characters**		59
一、汉字知识 Knowledge about Chinese Characters		59
1. 汉字的笔画（5） Strokes of Chinese characters (5)		
㇄ ㇅ ㇆ ㇇		
2. 汉字的结构（1） Structures of Chinese characters (1)		
独体结构 Independent structure		
二、汉字认读与书写 The Recognition and Writing of Chinese Characters		59
第三部分 日常用语 **Daily Expressions**		60
第四部分 单元实训 **Unit Practical Training**		60
温度传感器检测 Testing of Temperature Sensors		60
第五部分 单元小结 **Unit Summary**		61

第六单元　电路图识读　Unit 6　Interpretation of Circuit Diagrams　63

第一部分　课文　Texts　64
　　一、热身 Warm-up　64
　　二、课文 Texts　66
　　三、视听说 Viewing, Listening and Speaking　69
　　四、学以致用 Practicing What You Have Learnt　70
　　五、小知识 Tips　71

第二部分　汉字　Chinese Characters　71
　　一、汉字知识 Knowledge about Chinese Characters　71
　　　　1. 汉字的笔画（6）　Strokes of Chinese characters (6)
　　　　　　ㄋ　ㄢ
　　　　2. 汉字的结构（2）　Structures of Chinese characters (2)
　　　　　　品字形结构　品-shaped structure
　　二、汉字认读与书写 The Recognition and Writing of Chinese Characters　72

第三部分　日常用语　Daily Expressions　72
第四部分　单元实训　Unit Practical Training　72
　　电路图识图 Recognition of Circuit Diagrams　72
第五部分　单元小结　Unit Summary　73

第七单元　充电系统　Unit 7　Charging Systems　77

第一部分　课文　Texts　78
　　一、热身 Warm-up　78
　　二、课文 Texts　80
　　三、视听说 Viewing, Listening and Speaking　82
　　四、学以致用 Practicing What You Have Learnt　83
　　五、小知识 Tips　84

第二部分　汉字　Chinese Characters　85
　　一、汉字知识 Knowledge about Chinese Characters　85
　　　　1. 汉字的笔画（7）　Strokes of Chinese characters (7)
　　　　　　ㄅ　ㄟ
　　　　2. 汉字的结构（3）　Structures of Chinese characters (3)
　　　　　　上下结构 Top-bottom structure
　　　　　　上中下结构 Top-middle-bottom structure
　　二、汉字认读与书写 The Recognition and Writing of Chinese Characters　85

第三部分　日常用语　Daily Expressions　85

第四部分 单元实训	**Unit Practical Training**	86
电动汽车充电	Charging of Electric Vehicles	86
第五部分 单元小结	**Unit Summary**	87

第八单元　动力蓄电池拆装　Unit 8　Disassembly and Assembly of Power Storage Batteries　89

第一部分 课文	**Texts**	90
一、热身	Warm-up	90
二、课文	Texts	92
三、视听说	Viewing, Listening and Speaking	94
四、学以致用	Practicing What You Have Learnt	97
五、小知识	Tips	99
第二部分 汉字	**Chinese Characters**	100
一、汉字知识	Knowledge about Chinese Characters	100
1. 汉字的笔画（8）	Strokes of Chinese characters (8)	
乚　乁		
2. 汉字的结构（4）	Structures of Chinese characters (4)	
左右结构	Left-right structure	
左中右结构	Left-middle-right structure	
二、汉字认读与书写	The Recognition and Writing of Chinese Characters	100
第三部分 日常用语	**Daily Expressions**	101
第四部分 单元实训	**Unit Practical Training**	101
拆装电动汽车动力蓄电池		
	Disassembly and Assembly of Power Storage Batteries of Electric Vehicles	101
第五部分 单元小结	**Unit Summary**	102

第九单元　电动汽车试验　Unit 9　Electric Vehicle Tests　105

第一部分 课文	**Texts**	106
一、热身	Warm-up	106
二、课文	Texts	108
三、视听说	Viewing, Listening and Speaking	111
四、学以致用	Practicing What You Have Learnt	113
五、小知识	Tips	114

第二部分 汉字	**Chinese Characters**	115
一、汉字知识 Knowledge about Chinese Characters		115

    1. 汉字的笔画（9） Strokes of Chinese characters (9)

      ㇆ ㇈

    2. 汉字的结构（5） Structures of Chinese characters (5)

      全包围结构 Fully-enclosed structure

      半包围结构 Semi-enclosed structure

二、汉字认读与书写 The Recognition and Writing of Chinese Characters		115
第三部分 日常用语	**Daily Expressions**	115
第四部分 单元实训	**Unit Practical Training**	116
电动汽车基本试验 Basic Tests of Electric Vehicles		116
第五部分 单元小结	**Unit Summary**	117

第十单元　电动汽车销售　Unit 10　Electric Vehicle Sales　119

第一部分 课文	**Texts**	120
一、热身 Warm-up		120
二、课文 Texts		121
三、视听说 Viewing, Listening and Speaking		125
四、学以致用 Practicing What You Have Learnt		126
五、小知识 Tips		127
第二部分 汉字	**Chinese Characters**	128
一、汉字知识 Knowledge about Chinese Characters		128

    1. 汉字的笔画（总表） Strokes of Chinese characters (general table)

    2. 汉字的笔顺（总表） Stroke orders of Chinese characters (general table)

    3. 汉字的结构（总表） Structures of Chinese characters (general table)

二、汉字认读与书写 The Recognition and Writing of Chinese Characters		129
第三部分 日常用语	**Daily Expressions**	129
第四部分 单元实训	**Unit Practical Training**	129
模拟推荐电动汽车 Simulated Recommendation of Electric Vehicles		129
第五部分 单元小结	**Unit Summary**	130

附录　Appendixes　133

词汇总表	**Vocabulary**	133
视频脚本	**Video Scripts**	144
参考答案	**Reference Answers**	148

VI

1

Diàndòng qìchē jiǎnjiè
电动汽车简介
Introduction to Electric Vehicles

diàndòng qìchē zhǔyào bùjiàn
电动 汽车主要部件
main components of an electric vehicle

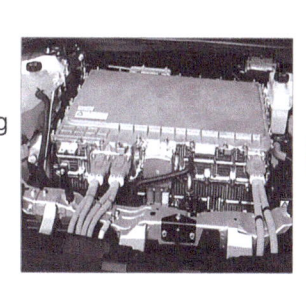

gāoyā diànkòng zǒngchéng
高压 电控　总成
high-voltage electronic control assembly

dīyā diànchí
低压电池
low-voltage battery

qūdòng diànjī
驱动 电机
driving motor

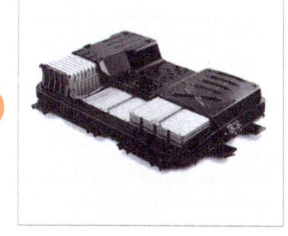

dònglì xùdiànchí
动力蓄电池
power storage battery

chōngdiànkǒu
充电口
charging port

chōngdiànzhuāng
充电桩
charging station

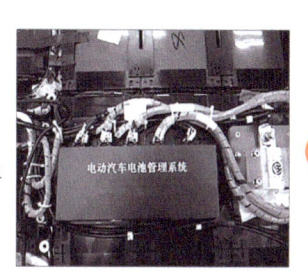

diànchí guǎnlǐ xìtǒng
电池管理系统
battery management system

1

题解 Introduction

1. 学习内容：电动汽车特点、结构及工作原理。
   Learning content: The characteristics, structure and working principle of electric vehicles
2. 知识目标：掌握电动汽车介绍相关核心词汇，了解汉字的笔画 "一" "丨" "丿" "㇏"、笔顺 "先横后竖、先撇后捺"，学写相关汉字。
   Knowledge objectives: To master the core vocabulary related to the introduction to electric vehicles, learn the strokes "一", "丨", "丿", "㇏" and the stroke orders "horizontal strokes before vertical strokes", and "left-falling strokes before right-falling strokes" of Chinese characters, and write the related characters
3. 技能目标：熟悉电动汽车主要部件及组成，掌握电动汽车电气工作原理。
   Skill objective: To be familiar with the main parts and components of electric vehicles and master the electrical working principle of electric vehicles

第一部分　Part 1

课文　Texts

一、热身　rèshēn　Warm-up

1. 给词语选择对应的图片。**Choose the corresponding pictures for the words.**

A.

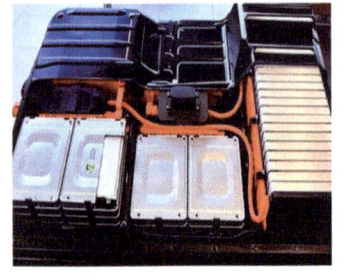

B.

C.

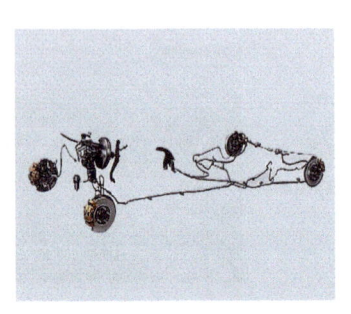

D.

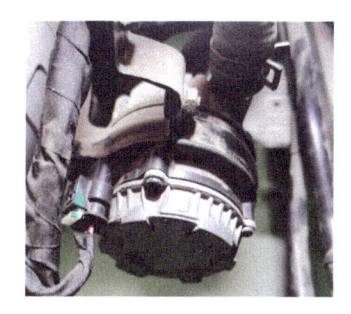

电动汽车简介 1
Introduction to Electric Vehicles

E.　　　　　　　　　　　　　　　F.

① dònglì diànchí xìtǒng
　动力电池系统＿＿＿＿＿＿＿＿
　power battery system

② zhuǎnxiàng xìtǒng
　转向系统＿＿＿＿＿＿＿＿
　steering system

③ zhìdòng xìtǒng
　制动系统＿＿＿＿＿＿＿＿
　braking system

④ dònglì diànjī xìtǒng
　动力电机系统＿＿＿＿＿＿＿＿
　power motor system

⑤ gāoyā pèidiàn xìtǒng
　高压配电系统＿＿＿＿＿＿＿＿
　high-voltage power distribution system

⑥ lěngquè xìtǒng
　冷却系统＿＿＿＿＿＿＿＿
　cooling system

2. 看视频，掌握电动汽车主要部件，观察下面车的结构，并在部件的位置填上对应的序号。**Watch the video, master the main components of an electric vehicle. Observe the structure of the vehicle below, and fill in the corresponding serial number in the position of the component.**

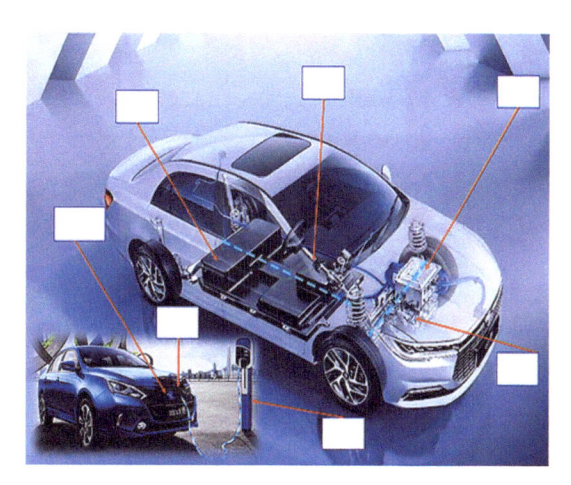

diàndòng qìchē zhǔyào bùjiàn
电动汽车主要部件
Main Components of an Electric Vehicle

3

A. 动力蓄电池 dònglì xùdiànchí
power storage battery

B. 高压电控总成 gāoyā diànkòng zǒngchéng
high-voltage electronic control assembly

C. 驱动电机 qūdòng diànjī
driving motor

D. 转向系统 zhuǎnxiàng xìtǒng
steering system

E. 充电口 chōngdiànkǒu
charging port

F. 充电桩 chōngdiànzhuāng
charging station

G. 充电插头 chōngdiàn chātóu
charging plug

二、课文 kèwén Texts

A 01-01

徒弟：师傅，电动汽车是指哪些车辆？有什么特点？

师傅：电动汽车是以车载电源为动力，用电机驱动车轮行驶的车辆。纯电动汽车的特点是依靠电力驱动，零排放，噪声低。

徒弟：电动汽车由哪些部分组成？

师傅：电动汽车主要由低压配电系统，高压电控系统，动力电机系统，动力电池系统，冷却、制动及转向系统组成。

译文 yìwén Text in English

Apprentice: Master, what vehicles are electric vehicles? What are the characteristics?

Master: An electric vehicle is a vehicle powered by an on-board power supply and using a motor to drive the wheels. Pure electric vehicles are characterized by relying on electric drive, zero emissions, and low noise.

Apprentice: What are the components of electric vehicles?

Master: Electric vehicles are mainly composed of low-voltage power distribution system, high-voltage electronic control system, power motor system, power battery system, as well as cooling, braking and steering systems.

普通词语 pǔtōng cíyǔ General Vocabulary 01-02

1.	指	zhǐ	v.	refer to
2.	车辆	chēliàng	n.	vehicle

3.	特点	tèdiǎn	n.	characteristic
4.	为	wéi	v.	act as
5.	纯	chún	adj.	pure
6.	依靠	yīkào	v.	depend on, rely on
7.	零	líng	num.	zero
8.	噪声	zàoshēng	n.	noise
9.	低	dī	adj.	low

专业词语 zhuānyè cíyǔ Specialized Vocabulary 01-03

1.	车载电源	chēzài diànyuán	phr.	on-board power supply
2.	车轮	chēlún	n.	wheel
3.	电力	diànlì	n.	electric power
4.	排放	páifàng	v.	emit
5.	低压配电系统	dīyā pèidiàn xìtǒng	phr.	low-voltage power distribution system
6.	高压电控系统	gāoyā diànkòng xìtǒng	phr.	high-voltage electronic control system
7.	动力电机系统	dònglì diànjī xìtǒng	phr.	power motor system
8.	动力电池系统	dònglì diànchí xìtǒng	phr.	power battery system

B 01-04

徒弟：师傅，动力电池系统包括哪些？

师傅：动力电池系统包括动力电池和电池管理系统。

徒弟：电动汽车是如何充电的呢？

师傅：需要充电桩、充电口和充电枪。充电口在车身上，充电枪可以位于车上，也可以位于充电桩上。

徒弟：高压电控总成、低压电池和驱动电机在哪里呢？它们是如何工作的？

shīfu: Tāmen tōngcháng zài qián yǐnqínggài li. Dīyā diànchí xiān gōng diàn, gāoyā diànkòng
师傅：他们 通常 在前 引擎盖里。低压电池 先供 电，高压电控
zǒngchéng shàng diàn zhīhòu, qūdòng diànjī zhuàndòng, qūdòng chēliàng xíngshǐ.
总成 上 电之后， 驱动电机 转动， 驱动 车辆 行驶。

译文 yìwén Text in English

Apprentice: Master, what does the power battery system include?

Master: Power battery system includes power battery and battery management system.

Apprentice: How are electric vehicles charged?

Master: You need a charging station, a charging port and a charging gun. The charging port is on the car body, and the charging gun can be located either on the car or on the charging station.

Apprentice: Where are the high-voltage electronic control assembly, low-voltage battery and driving motor located? How do they work?

Master: They are usually in the hood. The low-voltage battery provides power first. After the high-voltage electronic control assembly is powered on, the driving motor rotates to drive the vehicle.

普通词语 pǔtōng cíyǔ General Vocabulary 🎧 01-05

1.	管理	guǎnlǐ	v.	manage
2.	如何	rúhé	pron.	how
3.	呢	ne	part.	used at the end of a question
4.	位于	wèiyú	v.	locate
5.	通常	tōngcháng	adv.	usually

专业词语 zhuānyè cíyǔ Specialized Vocabulary 🎧 01-06

1.	充电桩	chōngdiànzhuāng	n.	charging station
2.	充电口	chōngdiànkǒu	n.	charging port
3.	充电枪	chōngdiànqiāng	n.	charging gun
4.	高压电控总成	gāoyā diànkòng zǒngchéng	phr.	high-voltage electronic control assembly
5.	低压电池	dīyā diànchí	phr.	low-voltage battery
6.	驱动电机	qūdòng diànjī	phr.	driving motor
7.	引擎盖	yǐnqínggài	n.	hood
8.	供	gōng	v.	provide
9.	转动	zhuàndòng	v.	rotate

电动汽车简介 1
Introduction to Electric Vehicles

三、视听说　shì-tīng-shuō　Viewing, Listening and Speaking

观看师傅向徒弟介绍电动汽车零部件的视频，将所听到的部件名称写在对应图片下面的横线上，再说出你所知道的电动汽车构成部件。**Watch the video of the master introducing electric vehicle components to the apprentice, mark the names of the components you have heard on the lines under the corresponding pictures, and then talk about the electric vehicle components you know.**

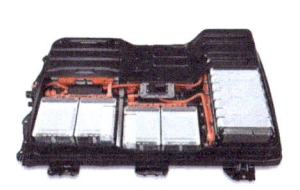

❶ _____

❷ _____

❸ _____

❹ _____

❺ _____

❻ _____

❼ _____

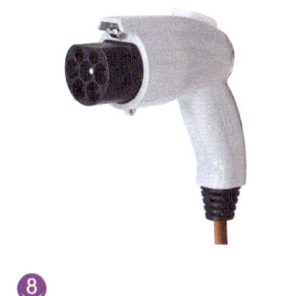

❽ _____

chōngdiànkǒu
A. 充电口
charging port

chōngdiànzhuāng
B. 充电桩
charging station

chōngdiànqiāng
C. 充电枪
charging gun

dīyā diànchí
D. 低压电池
low-voltage battery

gāoyā diànkòng zǒngchéng
E. 高压 电控 总成
high-voltage electronic control assembly

qūdòng diànjī
F. 驱动电机
driving motor

dònglì xùdiànchí
G. 动力蓄电池
power storage battery

diànchí guǎnlǐ xìtǒng
H. 电池管理系统
battery management system

四、学以致用　xuéyǐzhìyòng　Practicing What You Have Learnt

观看视频，听师傅向徒弟讲解高压电控总成、低压电池和动力电机的工作流程，将流程填在对应序号下的横线上，并尝试说出工作流程。**Watch the video and listen to the master explaining the working process of high-voltage electronic control assembly, low-voltage battery and power motor. Fill in the processes on the lines under the corresponding serial numbers, and try to tell the working process.**

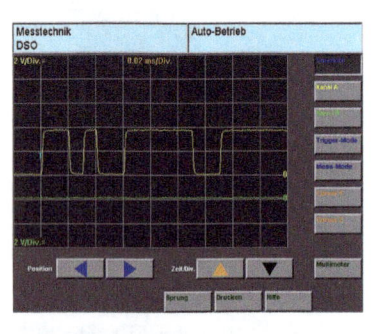

diàndòng　qìchē　shàng diàn
电动汽车上电
Power Up Electric Vehicles

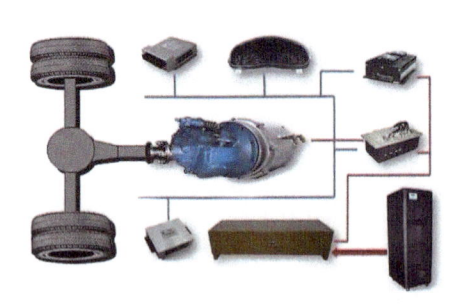

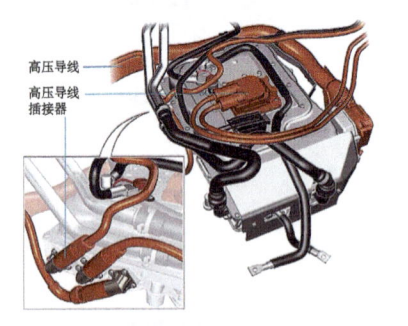

1　2　3

gāoyā diànkòn zǒngchéng shàng diàn
A. 高压 电控 总成 上 电
high-voltage control assembly powers up

B. 驱动电机 转动，驱动 车辆 行驶
   the driving motor rotates to drive the vehicle

C. 低压电池 供 电
   low-voltage battery supplies power

五、小知识 xiǎozhīshi Tips

电动 汽车 工作 原理
Diàndòng qìchē gōngzuò yuánlǐ

一款 纯 电动 汽车的 工作原理如下图所示，蓝色线是低压通信线，红色线为高压动力线。电机控制器将动力电池包的电能传递给驱动电机，再通过 变速箱 驱动 前轮行驶。电机控制器连接整车 CAN 总线，可以与中央 控制 单元、数字仪表板、动力电池管理系统进行通信。

Working Principle of Electric Vehicles

The working principle of a pure electric vehicle is shown in the figure below. The blue line is the low-voltage communication line, and the red line is the high-voltage power line. The motor controller transfers the electric energy of the power battery pack to the driving motor, and drives the front wheels to travel through the gearbox. The motor controller is connected to the vehicle CAN bus and can communicate with the central control unit, digital instrument panel, and power battery management system.

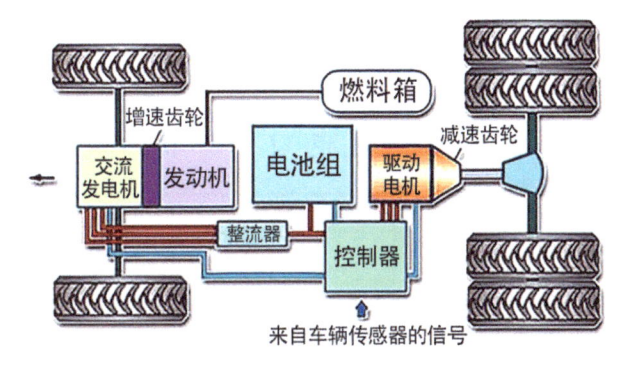

补充专业词语 bǔchōng zhuānyè cíyǔ Supplementary Specialized Vocabulary				01-07
1.	低压通信线	dīyā tōngxìnxiàn	phr.	low-voltage communication line
2.	高压动力线	gāoyā dònglìxiàn	phr.	high-voltage power line
3.	变速箱	biànsùxiāng	n.	gearbox

第二部分 Part 2 汉字 Chinese Characters

一、汉字知识 Hànzì zhīshi Knowledge about Chinese Characters

1. 汉字的笔画（1）Strokes of Chinese characters (1)

笔画 Strokes	名称 Names	例字 Examples
一	横 héng	二
丨	竖 shù	十
丿	撇 piě	人
乀	捺 nà	八

2. 汉字的笔顺（1）Stroke orders of Chinese characters (1)

规则 Rules	例字 Examples	笔顺 Stroke orders
先横后竖 Horizontal strokes before vertical strokes	十	一 十
先撇后捺 Left-falling strokes before right-falling strokes	人 八	丿 人 丿 八

二、汉字认读与书写 Hànzì rèndú yǔ shūxiě The Recognition and Writing of Chinese Characters

认读下列词语，并试着读写构成词语的汉字。
Recognize the following words, and try to read and write the Chinese characters forming these words.

车载电源　　充电口　　低压电池

车				载				电				源			
充				电				口				池			
低				压				电				池			

10

第三部分 Part 3 日常用语 Daily Expressions

❶ 劳驾，帮我叫辆出租车！ Láojià, bāng wǒ jiào liàng chūzūchē! Excuse me, please get me a taxi.
❷ 明天见。Míngtiān jiàn. See you tomorrow!
❸ 不见不散。Bújiàn-búsàn. Be there or be square!

第四部分 Part 4 单元实训 Unit Practical Training

动力电池充电故障排除
Power Battery Charging Troubleshooting

实训目的 Training purpose

通过实训，实训人员能够掌握动力电池充电故障，警告灯闪亮的故障排除方法。

Through the practical training, the trainees are able to master the troubleshooting methods of power battery charging failure and flashing warning lights.

实训组织 Training organization

每组 4 人

four trainees in each group

实训步骤 Training steps

❶ 教师带领学员围绕在故障车旁边，确认故障现象是否为不能为动力电池充电故障，警告灯闪亮。

The teacher leads the trainees around the faulty car and confirms whether the fault phenomenon is that the power battery cannot be charged, and the warning light is flashing.

❷ 将实训人员分成若干小组，每组 4 人。

Divide the trainees into groups of 4.

❸ 每组学员讨论并找出故障位置。

Each group of trainees discuss and find out the faulty location.

❹ 教师确认故障为充电电路有故障。

The teacher confirms that the fault is that the charging circuit is faulty.

❺ 教师指导学员进行故障排除：

The teacher guides the trainees to troubleshoot:

- 测量输入电压是否在 170V～260V 之间；
- Measure whether the input voltage is between 170V-260V;
- 检查充电桩与充电枪的连接是否正常；
- Check whether the connection between the charging station and the charging gun is normal;
- 充电线是否过细，若直径小于 2.5mm，更换充电桩及满足条件的电线。
- Whether the charging cable is too thin, if the diameter is less than 2.5mm, change the charging

station and replace the charging cable with one that meets the requirements.

❻ 学员进行故障排除练习。

The trainees carry out troubleshooting exercises.

❼ 教师总结评价，实训结束。

The teacher summarizes and evaluates, and the training ends.

第五部分　Part 5　单元小结　Unit Summary

cíyǔ 词语 Vocabulary

普通词语　General Vocabulary

1.	指	zhǐ	v.	refer to
2.	车辆	chēliàng	n.	vehicle
3.	特点	tèdiǎn	n.	characteristic
4.	为	wéi	v.	act as
5.	纯	chún	adj.	pure
6.	依靠	yīkào	v.	depend on, rely on
7.	零	líng	num.	zero
8.	噪声	zàoshēng	n.	noise
9.	低	dī	adj.	low
10.	管理	guǎnlǐ	v.	manage
11.	如何	rúhé	pron.	how
12.	呢	ne	part.	*used at the end of a question*
13.	位于	wèiyú	v.	locate
14.	通常	tōngcháng	adv.	usually

专业词语　Specialized Vocabulary

1.	车载电源	chēzài diànyuán	phr.	on-board power supply
2.	车轮	chēlún	n.	wheel
3.	电力	diànlì	n.	electric power
4.	排放	páifàng	v.	emit
5.	低压配电系统	dīyā pèidiàn xìtǒng	phr.	low-voltage power distribution system
6.	高压电控系统	gāoyā diànkòng xìtǒng	phr.	high-voltage electronic control system

电动汽车简介
Introduction to Electric Vehicles

cíyǔ 词语 Vocabulary

7.	动力电机系统	dònglì diànjī xìtǒng	phr.	power motor system
8.	动力电池系统	dònglì diànchí xìtǒng	phr.	power battery system
9.	充电桩	chōngdiàn zhuāng	n.	charging station
10.	充电口	chōngdiànkǒu	n.	charging port
11.	充电枪	chōngdiàn qiāng	n.	charging gun
12.	高压电控总成	gāoyā diànkòng zǒngchéng	phr.	high-voltage electronic control assembly
13.	低压电池	dīyā diànchí	phr.	low-voltage battery
14.	驱动电机	qūdòng diànjī	phr.	driving motor
15.	引擎盖	yǐnqínggài	n.	hood
16.	供	gōng	v.	provide
17.	转动	zhuàndòng	v.	rotate

补充专业词语 Supplementary Specialized Vocabulary

1.	低压通信线	dīyā tōngxìnxiàn	phr.	low-voltage communication line
2.	高压动力线	gāoyā dònglìxiàn	phr.	high-voltage power line
3.	变速箱	biànsùxiāng	n.	gearbox

jùzi 句子 Sentences

1. 电动汽车是以车载电源为动力，用电机驱动车轮行驶的车辆。纯电动汽车的特点是依靠电力驱动，零排放，噪声低。
2. 电动汽车主要由低压配电系统，高压电控系统，动力电机系统，动力电池系统，冷却、制动及转向系统组成。
3. 电动汽车充电需要充电桩、充电口和充电枪。充电口在车身上，充电枪可以位于车上，也可以位于充电桩上。

2

Diàndòng qìchē gāoyā diànkòng zǒngchéng
电动汽车高压电控 总成
High-voltage Electronic Control Assembly of Electric Vehicles

diàndòng qìchē
电动汽车
gāoyā diànkòng zǒngchéng
高压 电控 总成
high-voltage electronic control assembly of an electric vehicle

diànjī kòngzhìqì
电机控制器
motor controller

gāoyā kòngzhìhé
高压控制盒
high-voltage control box

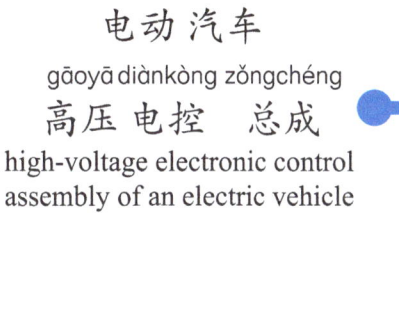

zhíliú biànyāqì
直流变压器
DC-to-DC converter

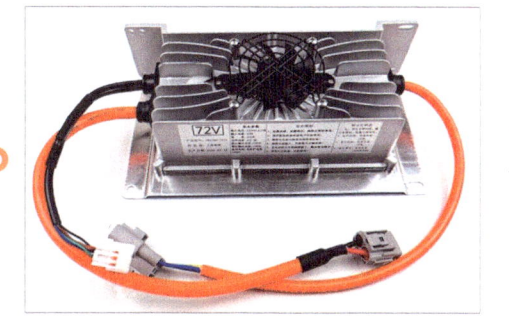

chēzài chōngdiànqì
车载 充电器
on-board charger

15

题解　Introduction

1. 学习内容：电动汽车高压电控总成的组成及工作原理。
   Learning content: The components and working principle of the high-voltage electronic control assembly of electric vehicles

2. 知识目标：掌握高压电控总成相关核心词汇，了解汉字的笔画 ""、""㇇""㇄""㇀"、笔顺"先上后下、先左后右"，学写相关汉字。
   Knowledge objectives: To master the core vocabulary related to the high-voltage electronic control assembly, learn the strokes "、", "㇇", "㇄", "㇀" and the stroke orders "upper strokes before lower strokes", and "left-side strokes before right-side strokes" of Chinese characters, and write the related characters

3. 技能目标：熟悉电动汽车高压电控总成的位置和接口作用，使用合适的方式给电动汽车充电。
   Skill objective: To be familiar with the position of the high-voltage electronic control assembly of electric vehicles and the functions of the interfaces, and use the appropriate method to charge electric vehicles

---

第一部分　Part 1

课文　Texts

一、热身　rèshēn　Warm-up

1. 给词语选择对应的图片。Choose the corresponding pictures for the words.

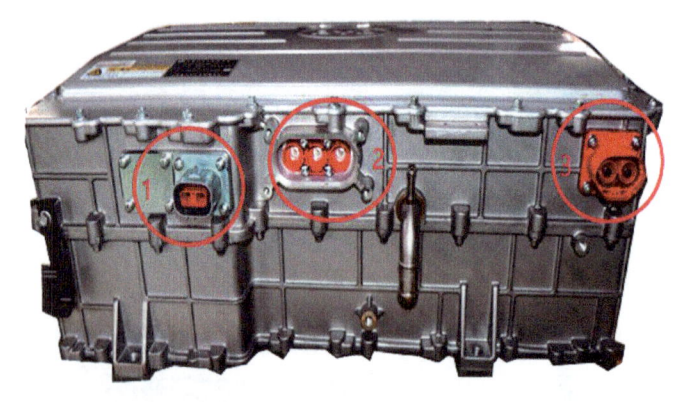

A. zhíliú chōngdiàn jiēkǒu
   直流充电接口
   DC charging interface
   （1）_____

B. jiāoliú chōngdiàn jiēkǒu
   交流充电接口
   AC charging interface
   （2）_____

C. qūdòng diànjī jiēkǒu
   驱动电机接口
   driving motor interface
   （3）_____

电动汽车高压电控总成 2

High-voltage Electronic Control Assembly of Electric Vehicles

2. 看视频，认识电动汽车高压电控总成，了解其正面接口的作用，将对应图片的序号填入括号中。

Watch the video to get to know the high-voltage electronic control assembly of electric vehicles and understand the function of its front interfaces. Fill the serial numbers of the corresponding pictures in the brackets.

比亚迪 e5 电动汽车"四合一"认知
Recognition of the "Four-In-One" of the BYD e5 Electric Vehicle

A.

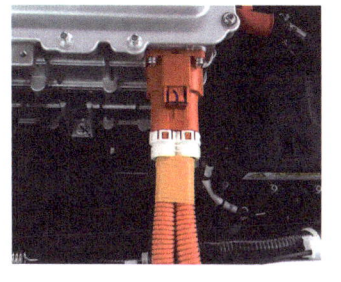

B.

C.

D.

（1）直流输入　　　　　　　　　　　　　　　　　　　　　　　（　　）
　　　DC input

（2）交流输入　　　　　　　　　　　　　　　　　　　　　　　（　　）
　　　AC input

（3）高压电控总成　　　　　　　　　　　　　　　　　　　　　（　　）
　　　high-voltage electronic control assembly

（4）三相交流输出　　　　　　　　　　　　　　　　　　　　　（　　）
　　　three-phase AC output

17

二、课文 kèwén Texts

A 02-01

shīfu: Jīntiān wǒmen lái xuéxí diàndòng qìchē gāoyā diànkòng zǒngchéng.
师傅：今天我们来学习电动汽车高压电控总成。

túdi: Gāoyā diànkòng zǒngchéng shì bu shì yòu bèi chēngwéi "sì hé yī"?
徒弟：高压电控总成是不是又被称为"四合一"？

shīfu: Shìde, tā jíchéngle diànjī kòngzhìqì、gāoyā kòngzhìhé、zhíliú biànyāqì hé chēzài chōngdiànqì.
师傅：是的，它集成了电机控制器、高压控制盒、直流变压器和车载充电器。

túdi: Gāoyā diànkòng zǒngchéng zài qìchē de shénme wèizhì?
徒弟：高压电控总成在汽车的什么位置？

shīfu: Wǒmen dǎkāi qìchē qián jīcāng, nǐ kàn, jiù zài zhèli. Jìzhùle, gāoyā diànkòng zǒngchéng yìbān bù yǔnxǔ chāijiě.
师傅：我们打开汽车前机舱，你看，就在这里。记住了，高压电控总成一般不允许拆解。

译文 yìwén Text in English

Master: Today we are going to learn the high-voltage electronic control assembly of electric vehicles.
Apprentice: Is the high-voltage electronic control assembly also called "four-in-one"?
Master: Yes. It integrates the motor controller, high-voltage control box, DC-to-DC converter and on-board charger.
Apprentice: Where is the high-voltage electronic control assembly located in a vehicle?
Master: Let's open the front hood. Look, it's right here. Remember that the high-voltage electronic control assembly is generally not allowed to be disassembled.

普通词语 pǔtōng cíyǔ General Vocabulary 02-02

1.	又	yòu	adv.	also
2.	被	bèi	part.	used in a passive sentence to introduce the agent/doer
3.	称	chēng	v.	call, name
4.	前	qián	n.	front
5.	记住	jìzhù	v.	remember
6.	一般	yìbān	adv.	generally
7.	允许	yǔnxǔ	v.	allow

专业词语 zhuānyè cíyǔ Specialized Vocabulary 02-03

1.	集成	jíchéng	v.	integrate

18

2.	四合一	sì hé yī	phr.	four-in-one
3.	电机控制器	diànjī kòngzhìqì	phr.	motor controller
4.	高压控制盒	gāoyā kòngzhìhé	phr.	high-voltage control box
5.	直流变压器	zhíliú biànyāqì	phr.	DC-to-DC converter
6.	车载充电器	chēzài chōngdiànqì	phr.	on-board charger
7.	机舱	jīcāng	n.	engine room
8.	拆解	chāijiě	v.	disassemble

B 02-04

徒弟：师傅，高压电控总成的作用是什么？

师傅：每个组成部分的作用不同。电机控制器的作用是将动力蓄电池的直流电转化为合适的交流电，供给电机使用。车载充电器的作用是对蓄电池进行交流充电。

徒弟：好的，那直流变压器和高压控制盒呢？

师傅：直流变压器的作用是将直流高压变为直流低压。高压控制盒的作用是控制高压电路的输入和输出，检测高压漏电等。

译文 yìwén Text in English

Apprentice: Master, what is the function of the high-voltage electronic control assembly?

Master: Each component has different functions. The function of the motor controller is to convert the DC of the power storage battery into appropriate AC for the use of the motor. The function of the on-board charger is to charge the storage battery by AC.

Apprentice: OK. What about the DC-to-DC converter and high-voltage control box?

Master: The function of the DC-to-DC converter is to change high-voltage DC into low-voltage DC. The function of the high-voltage control box is to control the input and output of high-voltage circuit, detect high-voltage leakage, etc.

普通词语 pǔtōng cíyǔ General Vocabulary   🎧 02-05

1.	转化	zhuǎnhuà	v.	convert
2.	合适	héshì	adj.	appropriate, suitable
3.	进行	jìnxíng	v.	proceed
4.	控制	kòngzhì	v.	control
5.	等	děng	part.	etc., and so on

专业词语 zhuānyè cíyǔ Specialized Vocabulary   🎧 02-06

1.	直流	zhíliú	n.	DC, direct current
2.	交流	jiāoliú	n.	AC, alternating current
3.	电路	diànlù	n.	circuit
4.	输入	shūrù	v.	input
5.	输出	shūchū	v.	output
6.	检测	jiǎncè	v.	detect
7.	漏电	lòudiàn	v.	(of electricity) leak

三、视听说 shì-tīng-shuō Viewing, Listening and Speaking

1. 观看介绍高压电控总成各组成部分工作原理的相关视频，将高压电控总成各部分名称写在对应的横线上，并尝试说出其工作原理。**Watch the related video introducing the working principle of the components of the high-voltage electronic control assembly, fill in the names of the components of the high-voltage electronic control assembly on the corresponding lines, and try to tell its working principle.**

高压电控总成认知
Recognition of the High-voltage Electronic Control Assembly

A. 车载 充电器
chēzài chōngdiànqì
on-board charger

B. DC/DC
DC/DC
DC-to-DC converter

电动汽车高压电控总成 2
High-voltage Electronic Control Assembly of Electric Vehicles

diànjī kòngzhìqì
C. 电机控制器
motor controller

gāoyā kòngzhìhé
D. 高压控制盒
high-voltage control box

Jiǎncè gāoyā diànliú hé lòudiàn qíngkuàng.
❶ 检测高压电流和漏电情况。_____
Detect situations with high-voltage current and leakage.

Kòngzhì qūdòng diànjī, shǐ chēliàng zhèngcháng xíngshǐ.
❷ 控制驱动电机，使车辆正常行驶。_____
Control the driving motor to allow the vehicle to run normally.

Gěi qìchē chōngdiàn.
❸ 给汽车充电。_____
Charge the vehicle.

Jiāng gāoyā biànwéi dīyā, gōng chēdēng děng dīyā diànqì shǐyòng.
❹ 将高压变为低压，供车灯等低压电器使用。_____
Convert high voltage into low voltage for the use of low-voltage appliances, such as vehicle lights.

2. 请说出电动汽车高压电控总成的工作原理。**Please tell the working principle of the high-voltage electronic control assembly of electric vehicles.**

四、学以致用　xuéyǐzhìyòng　Practicing What You Have Learnt

观看介绍电动汽车充电方式的相关视频，了解交流充电和直流充电的区别，判断在以下情况中应选用哪种方式充电。**Watch the related video introducing the charging methods of electric vehicles, learn about the differences between AC charging and DC charging, and judge which method should be used to charge in the following cases.**

diàndòng qìchē chōngdiàn fāngshì
电动汽车充电方式
Charging Methods of Electric Vehicles

21

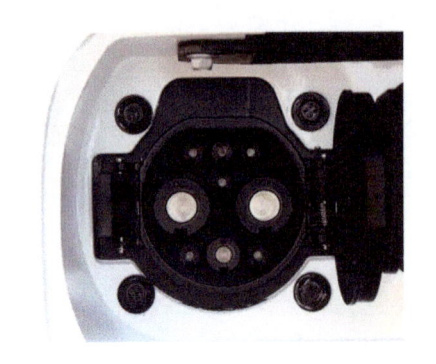

　　　　jiāoliú chōngdiàn　　　　　　　　zhíliú chōngdiàn
A. 交流充电　　　　　　　　　　B. 直流充电
　　AC charging　　　　　　　　　　　DC charging

　　zháojí chū yuǎnmén
① 着急出远门 go for a long journey in a hurry　　　　　　　　　　（　　）

　　zài jiāli chōngdiàn
② 在家里充电 charge at home　　　　　　　　　　　　　　　　　（　　）

　　yáncháng diànchí shòumìng
③ 延长电池寿命 extend battery life　　　　　　　　　　　　　　（　　）

五、小知识　xiǎozhīshi　Tips

　　　　　　　　　　Shénme shì "zǒngchéng"?
　　　　　　　　　什么是"总成"？

　　　　"Zǒngchéng" shì jīxiè lǐngyù lǐmiàn de chángyòng míngcí.　Yíxìliè língjiàn huòzhě chǎnpǐn,
　　　"总成"是机械领域里面的常用名词。一系列零件或者产品，

zǔchéng yí gè shíxiàn mǒu gè tèdìng gōngnéng de zhěngtǐ,　jí wéi zǒngchéng.
组成一个实现某个特定功能的整体，即为总成。

　　　Zài qìchē chǎnyè zhōng, tōngcháng bǎ gè zǒngchéng zuòwéi dúlì de jiégòu dānyuán lái zǔzhī
　　在汽车产业中，通常把各总成作为独立的结构单元来组织

shēngchǎn. Zài qìchē xiūlǐ zhōng, yǒushí zhíjiē bǎ mǒu yí gè zǒngchéng cóng qìchē shang chāi xia-
生产。在汽车修理中，有时直接把某一个总成从汽车上拆下

lai, huànshàng xīn de huò jīngguò xiūlǐ bìng jiǎnyàn hégé de
来，换上新的或经过修理并检验合格的

zǒngchéng, cóng'ér suōduǎnle qìchē xiūlǐ de shíjiān, tí-
总成，从而缩短了汽车修理的时间，提

gāole xiūlǐ zhìliàng.
高了修理质量。

22

电动汽车高压电控总成
High-voltage Electronic Control Assembly of Electric Vehicles

What Is "Assembly"?

"Assembly" is a common term in the field of machinery. A series of parts or products form a whole that realizes a specific function, namely assembly.

In auto industry, each assembly is usually manufactured as an independent structural unit. In auto repair, a certain assembly is sometimes removed from the vehicle directly and replaced with a new or repaired and qualified assembly, thus shortening the time of auto repair and improving the repair quality.

补充专业词语 bǔchōng zhuānyè cíyǔ Supplementary Specialized Vocabulary 🎧 02-07

1.	电流	diànliú	n.	electric current
2.	寿命	shòumìng	n.	life, lifespan
3.	机械	jīxiè	n.	machinery
4.	结构单元	jiégòu dānyuán	phr.	structural unit
5.	生产	shēngchǎn	v.	manufacture
6.	合格	hégé	adj.	qualified

第二部分 Part 2 汉字 Chinese Characters

一、汉字知识 Hànzì zhīshi Knowledge about Chinese Characters

1. 汉字的笔画（2） Strokes of Chinese characters (2)

笔画 Strokes	名称 Names	例字 Examples
丶	点 diǎn	六
乛	横折 héngzhé	口、日、五
ㄴ	竖折 shùzhé	山
ㄥ	撇折 piězhé	幺

2. 汉字的笔顺（2） Stroke orders of Chinese characters (2)

规则 Rules	例字 Examples	笔顺 Stroke orders
先上后下 Upper strokes before lower strokes	三	一 二 三
先左后右 Left-side strokes before right-side strokes	人	丿 人

23

二、汉字认读与书写　Hànzì rèndú yǔ shūxiě　The Recognition and Writing of Chinese Characters

认读下列词语，并试着读写构成词语的汉字。
Recognize the following words, and try to read and write the Chinese characters forming these words.

高压电控总成　　转化　　允许　　输入

高			压			电			控		
总			成			转			化		
允			许			输			入		

第三部分　Part 3　日常用语 Daily Expressions

❶ 你是学生吗？　Nǐ shì xuéshēng ma? Are you a student?

❷ 你爸爸做什么工作？　Nǐ bàba zuò shénme gōngzuò? What does your father do?

第四部分　Part 4　单元实训 Unit Practical Training

电动汽车高压电控总成
High-voltage Electronic Control Assembly of Electric Vehicles

实训目的 Training purpose

通过实训，实训人员能够熟悉电动汽车高压电控总成的位置和接口的作用，使用合适的方式给电动汽车充电。

Through the practical training, the trainees are able to familiarize themselves with the position of the high-voltage electronic control assembly of electric vehicles and the functions of the interfaces, and use the appropriate method to charge electric vehicles.

实训组织 Training organization

每组 4 人

four trainees in each group

实训步骤 Training steps

❶ 教师准备一台电动汽车和充电设备。

The teacher prepares an electric vehicle and charging equipment.

❷ 学员分组，每组 4 人。

Divide the trainees into groups of 4.

❸ 学员找到高压电控总成的位置，说出各接口的作用，选用合适的方式给汽车充电。

The trainees find the position of the high-voltage electronic control assembly, explain the function of each interface, and select an appropriate method to charge the vehicle.

❹ 学员互评。

The trainees carry out peer assessment.

❺ 教师总结评价，实训结束。

The teacher summarizes and evaluates, and the training ends.

第五部分　Part 5　单元小结 Unit Summary

cíyǔ 词语 Vocabulary

普通词语　General Vocabulary

1.	又	yòu	adv.	also
2.	被	bèi	part.	used in a passive sentence to introduce the agent/doer
3.	称	chēng	v.	call, name
4.	前	qián	n.	front
5.	记住	jìzhù	v.	remember
6.	一般	yìbān	adv.	generally
7.	允许	yǔnxǔ	v.	allow
8.	转化	zhuǎnhuà	v.	convert
9.	合适	héshì	adj.	appropriate, suitable
10.	进行	jìnxíng	v.	proceed
11.	控制	kòngzhì	v.	control
12.	等	děng	part.	etc., and so on

专业词语　Specialized Vocabulary

1.	集成	jíchéng	v.	integrate
2.	四合一	sì hé yī	phr.	four-in-one
3.	电机控制器	diànjī kòngzhìqì	phr.	motor controller
4.	高压控制盒	gāoyā kòngzhìhé	phr.	high-voltage control box

cíyǔ 词语 Vocabulary

5.	直流变压器	zhíliú biànyāqì	phr.	DC-to-DC converter
6.	车载充电器	chēzài chōngdiànqì	phr.	on-board charger
7.	机舱	jīcāng	n.	engine room
8.	拆解	chāijiě	v.	disassemble
9.	直流	zhíliú	n.	DC, direct current
10.	交流	jiāoliú	n.	AC, alternating current
11.	电路	diànlù	n.	circuit
12.	输入	shūrù	v.	input
13.	输出	shūchū	v.	output
14.	检测	jiǎncè	v.	detect
15.	漏电	lòudiàn	v.	(of electricity) leak

补充专业词语 Supplementary Specialized Vocabulary

1.	电流	diànliú	n.	electric current
2.	寿命	shòumìng	n.	life, lifespan
3.	机械	jīxiè	n.	machinery
4.	结构单元	jiégòu dānyuán	phr.	structural unit
5.	生产	shēngchǎn	v.	manufacture
6.	合格	hégé	adj.	qualified

jùzi 句子 Sentences

1. 电动汽车高压电控总成又称为"四合一",它集成了电机控制器、高压控制盒、直流变压器和车载充电器。
2. 电机控制器的作用是将动力蓄电池的直流电转化为合适的交流电,供给电机使用。
3. 车载充电器的作用是对蓄电池进行交流充电。
4. 直流变压器的作用是将直流高压变为直流低压。
5. 高压控制盒的作用是控制高压电路的输入和输出,检测高压漏电等。

3

Diàndòng qìchē juéyuán jiǎncè
电动汽车绝缘检测
Insulation Testing of Electric Vehicles

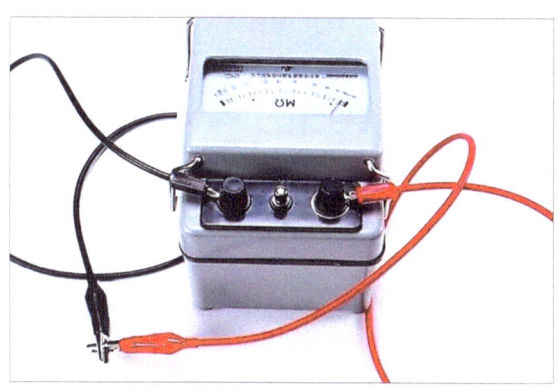

zhào'ōubiǎo zìjiǎn
兆欧表自检
the self testing of meggers

diàndòng qìchē juéyuán jiǎncè
电动汽车绝缘检测
insulation testing of electric vehicles

juéyuándiàn jiǎncè
绝缘垫检测
the testing of insulating mats

gāoyā bùjiàn jiǎncè
高压部件检测
the testing of high-voltage parts

27

题解　Introduction

1. 学习内容：电动汽车兆欧表自检、绝缘垫检测和高压部件绝缘检测。
   Learning content: The self testing of meggers, the testing of insulating mats and the insulation testing of high-voltage parts for electric vehicles
2. 知识目标：掌握电动汽车绝缘检测相关核心词汇，了解汉字的笔画"㇐""丨""丿""乚"、笔顺"先中间后两边、先外边后里边"，学写相关汉字。
   Knowledge objectives: To master the core vocabulary related to the insulation testing of electric vehicles, learn the strokes "㇐", "丨", "丿", "乚" and the stroke orders "strokes in the middle before those on both sides", and "outside strokes before inside strokes" of Chinese characters, and write the related characters
3. 技能目标：熟悉电动汽车的兆欧表自检、绝缘垫检测和高压部件检测，学会电动汽车绝缘检测。
   Skill objective: To be familiar with the self testing of meggers, the testing of insulating mats and the testing of high-voltage parts for electric vehicles, and learn the insulation testing of electric vehicles

第一部分　Part 1

课文　Texts

一、热身　rèshēn　Warm-up

1. 给词语选择对应的图片。Choose the corresponding pictures for the words.

A.

B.

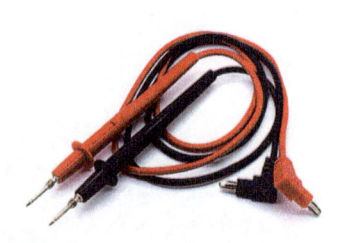

C.

D.

电动汽车绝缘检测
Insulation Testing of Electric Vehicles

3

E.

F.

① zhào'ōubiǎo
兆欧表_____
megger

② biǎobǐ
表笔_____
probe

③ juéyuándiàn
绝缘垫_____
insulating mat

④ kōngtiáo yāsuōjī
空调压缩机_____
air conditioning compressor

⑤ juéyuán gōngjù
绝缘工具_____
insulation tool

⑥ gélí hùlán
隔离护栏_____
isolation guard rail

2. 看视频，了解电动汽车绝缘检测的流程，选择各图片对应的流程。**Watch the video to learn about the process of the insulation testing of electric vehicles, and select the process corresponding to each picture.**

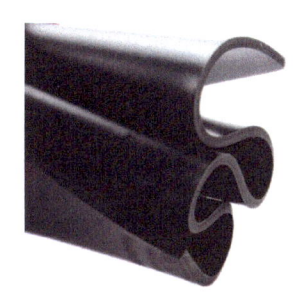

juéyuándiàn jiǎncè
A. 绝缘垫检测
the testing of insulating mats

gāoyā bùjiàn jiǎncè
B. 高压部件检测
the testing of high-voltage parts

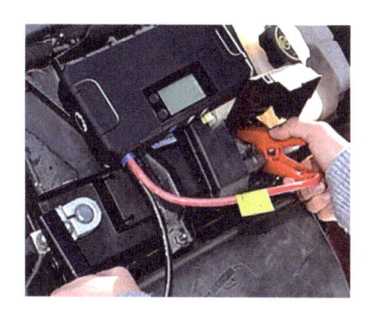

zhào'ōubiǎo zìjiǎn
C. 兆欧表自检
the self testing of meggers

（1）_____ ⟶ （2）_____ ⟶ （3）_____

29

二、课文　kèwén　Texts

A　03-01

徒弟：师傅，怎么检查兆欧表？

师傅：将红、黑表笔分开，按下开关按钮，选择"1000Ω"挡，按下"TEST"按钮，观察数值是否为"∞"。

徒弟：师傅，数值是"∞"。接下来做什么呢？

师傅：按下开关按钮断电，将红、黑表笔短接，按下开关按钮通电，选择"100Ω"挡，按下"TEST"按钮，观察数值是否为"0"。

徒弟：师傅，数值是"0"。

师傅：这两项都正常，说明兆欧表正常，可以使用。

译文　yìwén　Text in English

Apprentice: Master, how to check the megger?

Master: Separate the red and black probes, press the switch button, select "1000Ω" and press the "TEST" button to observe whether the value is "∞".

Apprentice: Master, the value is "∞". What shall I do next?

Master: Press the switch button to power off, short-circuit the red and black probes; press the switch button to power on, select "100Ω" and press the "TEST" button to observe whether the value is "0".

Apprentice: Master, the value is "0".

Master: These two items are normal, indicating that the megger is normal and can be used.

普通词语　pǔtōng cíyǔ　General Vocabulary　03-02

1.	检查	jiǎnchá	v.	check
2.	分开	fēnkāi	v.	separate
3.	按	àn	v.	press

4.	选择	xuǎnzé	v.	select
5.	观察	guānchá	v.	observe
6.	是否	shìfǒu	adv.	whether
7.	接下来	jiē xiàlái	phr.	next
8.	将	jiāng	prep.	used to introduce the object before the verb
9.	项	xiàng	m.	item
10.	说明	shuōmíng	v.	indicate, show
11.	正常	zhèngcháng	adj.	normal

专业词语 zhuānyè cíyǔ Specialized Vocabulary 03-03

1.	兆欧表	zhào'ōubiǎo	n.	megger
2.	表笔	biǎobǐ	n.	probe
3.	开关	kāiguān	n.	switch
4.	数值	shùzhí	n.	value
5.	断电	duàndiàn	phr.	power off
6.	短接	duǎnjiē	v.	short-circuit
7.	通电	tōngdiàn	phr.	power on

B 03-04

túdi: Shīfu, jiē xiàlái jiǎnchá shénme?
徒弟：师傅，接下来检查什么？

shīfu: Xiànzài wǒmen jiǎnchá juéyuándiàn. Yòng zhào'ōubiǎo cèliáng juéyuándiàn chē qián、chē hòu、chē zuǒ、chē yòu、chē zhōng 5 gè diǎn de juéyuán diànzǔ.
师傅：现在我们检查绝缘垫。用兆欧表测量绝缘垫车前、车后、车左、车右、车中5个点的绝缘电阻。

túdi: Zǔzhí duō dà shuōmíng juéyuán xìngnéng zhèngcháng?
徒弟：阻值多大说明绝缘性能正常？

shīfu: Dàyú 20 zhào'ōu.
师傅：大于20兆欧。

túdi: Hǎo de, míngbai le.
徒弟：好的，明白了。

shīfu: Lái, wǒmen kànxià gāoyā bùjiàn de juéyuán jiǎncè ba, tā bāokuò 9 gè bùjiàn ne.
师傅：来，我们看下高压部件的绝缘检测吧，它包括9个部件呢。

译文 yìwén Text in English

Apprentice: Master, what shall I check next?
Master: Now let's check the insulating mat. Use the megger to measure the insulation resistance of 5 points in the front, rear, left, right and central part of the insulating mat.
Apprentice: What resistance value indicates normal insulation performance?
Master: Larger than 20 megohms.
Apprentice: OK, I see.
Master: Now let's come to the insulation testing of high-voltage parts. It consists of nine parts.

普通词语 pǔtōng cíyǔ General Vocabulary 🎧 03-05

1.	大于	dàyú	v.	be greater/larger than

专业词语 zhuānyè cíyǔ Specialized Vocabulary 🎧 03-06

1.	绝缘垫	juéyuándiàn	n.	insulating mat
2.	绝缘电阻	juéyuán diànzǔ	phr.	insulation resistance
3.	阻值	zǔzhí	n.	resistance value
4.	绝缘性能	juéyuán xìngnéng	phr.	insulation performance

三、视听说 shì-tīng-shuō Viewing, Listening and Speaking

观看介绍高压部件绝缘检测流程的相关视频，说出不同高压部件对应的绝缘电阻值分别是多少，并连线。**Watch the related video introducing the process of the insulation testing of high-voltage parts, talk about the corresponding insulation resistance values of different high-voltage parts, and connect the pictures to the values.**

gāoyā bùjiàn juéyuán jiǎncè
高压部件绝缘检测
Insulation Testing of High-voltage Parts

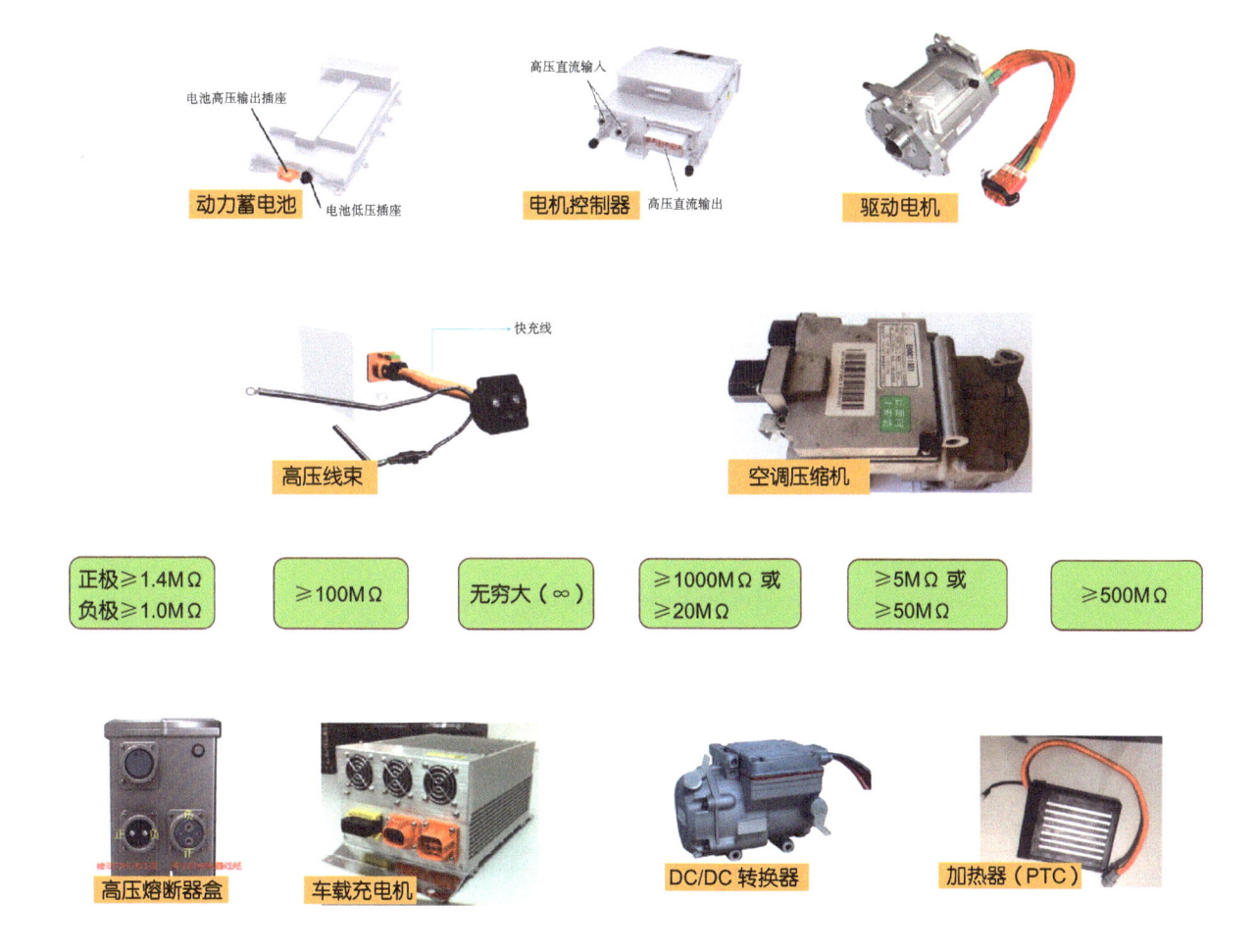

电动汽车绝缘检测 3
Insulation Testing of Electric Vehicles

电池高压输出插座	高压直流输入	
动力蓄电池 / 电池低压插座	电机控制器 / 高压直流输出	驱动电机

快充线	
高压线束	空调压缩机

| 正极≥1.4MΩ 负极≥1.0MΩ | ≥100MΩ | 无穷大(∞) | ≥1000MΩ 或 ≥20MΩ | ≥5MΩ 或 ≥50MΩ | ≥500MΩ |

| 高压熔断器盒 | 车载充电机 | DC/DC 转换器 | 加热器(PTC) |

四、学以致用　xuéyǐzhìyòng　**Practicing What You Have Learnt**

观看视频，判断该绝缘垫的哪些部位绝缘性能正常，哪些部位绝缘性能不正常。**Watch the video, and judge which parts of the insulating mat have normal insulation performance and which parts do not.**

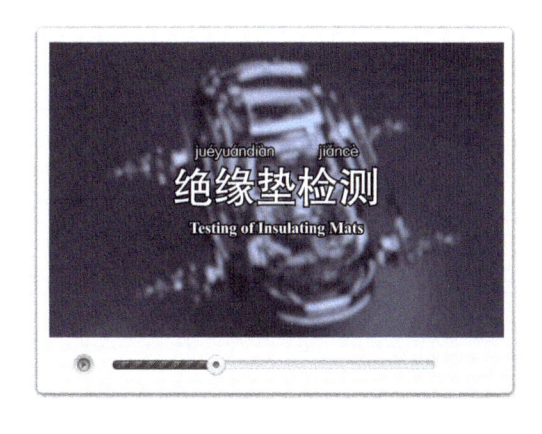

jué yuán diàn　jiǎn cè
绝缘垫检测
Testing of Insulating Mats

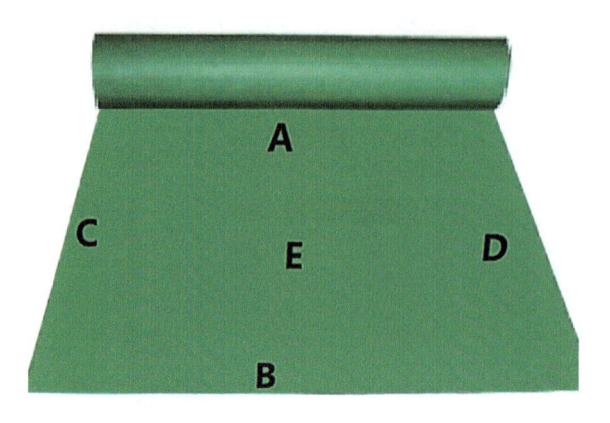

zhèngcháng bùwèi:
1. 正常 部位：＿＿＿＿＿＿

bú zhèngcháng bùwèi:
2. 不 正常 部位：＿＿＿＿＿＿

normal parts

abnormal parts

五、小知识　xiǎozhīshi　Tips

Diànliú duì réntǐ de zuòyòng
电流对人体的作用
The Effect of Electric Current on the Human Body

电流 diànliú electric current (mA)	作用 zuòyòng　effect	
	50~60Hz jiāoliúdiàn 50~60Hz 交流电 50~60 Hz alternating current	zhíliúdiàn 直流电 direct current
0.6~1.5	kāishǐ yǒu gǎnjué, shǒu qīngqīng chàndǒu 开始有感觉，手轻轻颤抖 starting to get the feel, with hands slightly trembling	wú gǎnjué 无感觉 insensible
2~3	shǒuzhǐ qiángliè chàndǒu 手指强烈颤抖 fingers trembling violently	wú gǎnjué 无感觉 insensible
5~7	shǒubù jìngluán 手部痉挛 hands being convulsed	gǎnjué yǎng hé rè 感觉痒和热 feeling itchy and hot
8~10	shǒuzhǐ jiàonán bǎituō diànjí, dàn hái néng bǎituō 手指较难摆脱电极，但还能摆脱 fingers being able to get rid of the electrodes but with difficulty	rè gǎnjué zēngqiáng 热感觉增强 feeling hotter
20~25	shǒu xùnsù mábì, bùnéng bǎituō diànjí 手迅速麻痹，不能摆脱电极 hands getting paralysed and being unable to get rid of the electrodes	rè gǎnjué dàdà zēngqiáng 热感觉大大增强 feeling hotter and hotter

（续表）

电流 diànliú electric current（mA）	作用 zuòyòng effect	
50~80	hūxī mábì, xīnfáng kāishǐ zhènchàn 呼吸麻痹，心房开始 震颤 having a respiratory paralysis and atrial tremors	qiángliè rè gǎnjué, hūxī kùnnan 强烈 热感觉，呼吸困难 feeling extremely hot, and having difficulty in breathing
90~100	hūxī mábì, yánxù 3 miǎo xīnzāng mábì 呼吸麻痹，延续 3 秒 心脏麻痹 having a respiratory paralysis with heart attack lasting for three seconds	hūxī mábì 呼吸麻痹 having a respiratory paralysis
300 yǐshàng 300 以上 over 300	zuòyè 0.1 miǎo, hūxī xīnzāng mábì, jītǐ 作业 0.1 秒，呼吸心脏 麻痹，肌体 zǔzhī pòhuài 组织 破坏 0.1 seconds operation, resulting in a respiratory paralysis, heart attack, and body tissue destruction	

补充专业词语 bǔchōng zhuānyè cíyǔ Supplementary Specialized Vocabulary 🎧 03-07

1. 流程　　　　liúchéng　　　　　　n.　　process, procedure
2. 正极　　　　zhèngjí　　　　　　　n.　　positive pole
3. 负极　　　　fùjí　　　　　　　　　n.　　negative pole
4. 空调压缩机　kōngtiáo yāsuōjī　　　phr.　air conditioning compressor
5. DC/DC 转换器　DC/DC zhuǎnhuànqì　phr.　DC-to-DC converter

第二部分　Part 2
汉字　Chinese Characters

一、汉字知识　Hànzì zhīshi　Knowledge about Chinese Characters

1. 汉字的笔画（3）Strokes of Chinese characters (3)

笔画 Strokes	名称 Names	例字 Examples
㇇	横钩 hénggōu	买
亅	竖钩 shùgōu	小
㇉	弯钩 wāngōu	子
㇄	竖弯钩 shùwāngōu	七

2. 汉字的笔顺（3） **Stroke orders of Chinese characters (3)**

规则 Rules	例字 Examples	笔顺 Stroke orders
先中间后两边 Strokes in the middle before those on both sides	小	亅 小 小
先外边后里边 Outside strokes before inside strokes	问	丶 冂 门 问 问 问

二、汉字认读与书写　　Hànzì rèndú yǔ shūxiě　　**The Recognition and Writing of Chinese Characters**

认读下列词语，并试着读写构成词语的汉字。
Recognize the following words, and try to read and write the Chinese characters forming these words.

检查　　绝缘　　电阻　　正常

| 检 | | | 查 | | | 绝 | | | 缘 | | |
| 电 | | | 阻 | | | 正 | | | 常 | | |

第三部分　Part 3
日常用语 Daily Expressions

❶ 我来介绍一下，这位是李伟先生。Wǒ lái jièshào yíxià, zhè wèi shì Lǐ Wěi xiānsheng. Let me introduce you. This is Mr. Li Wei.

❷ 请问，南京饭店在哪儿？ Qǐngwèn, Nánjīng Fàndiàn zài nǎr? Excuse me, where's Nanjing Hotel?

❸ 请问，这个汉语怎么说？ Qǐngwèn, zhège Hànyǔ zěnme shuō? Excuse me, what's this in Chinese?

第四部分　Part 4
单元实训 Unit Practical Training

电动汽车绝缘检测　Insulation Testing of Electric Vehicles

实训目的 Training purpose

通过实训，实训人员能够对电动汽车进行欧兆表自检、绝缘垫检测和高压部件检测。

Through the practical training, the trainees are able to conduct the self testing of meggers, the testing of insulating mats and the testing of high-voltage parts on electric vehicles.

实训组织 Training organization

每组 4 人

four trainees in each group

实训步骤 Training steps

❶ 兆欧表自检。

The self testing of meggers.

❷ 绝缘垫检测。

The insulation testing of insulating mats.

❸ 高压部件绝缘检测。

The insulation testing of high-voltage parts.

注：高压部件包含动力蓄电池、电机控制器、驱动电机、高压线束、空调压缩机、高压熔断器盒、车载充电机、DC/DC 转换器、加热器（PTC）等。

Note: The high-voltage parts include power storage battery, motor controller, driving motor, high-voltage wiring harness, air conditioning compressor, high-voltage fuse box, on-board charger, DC-to-DC converter, heater (PTC), etc.

❹ 学员互评。

The trainees carry out peer assessment.

❺ 教师总结评价，实训结束。

The teacher summarizes and evaluates, and the training ends.

第五部分　Part 5　单元小结 Unit Summary

词语 cíyǔ Vocabulary

普通词语　General Vocabulary

1.	检查	jiǎnchá	v.	check
2.	分开	fēnkāi	v.	separate
3.	按	àn	v.	press
4.	选择	xuǎnzé	v.	select
5.	观察	guānchá	v.	observe
6.	是否	shìfǒu	adv.	whether
7.	接下来	jiē xiàlái	phr.	next
8.	将	jiāng	prep.	*used to introduce the object before the verb*
9.	项	xiàng	m.	item
10.	说明	shuōmíng	v.	indicate, show

词语 Vocabulary

11.	正常	zhèngcháng	adj.	normal
12.	大于	dàyú	v.	be greater/larger than

专业词语　Specialized Vocabulary

1.	兆欧表	zhào'ōubiǎo	n.	megger
2.	表笔	biǎobǐ	n.	probe
3.	开关	kāiguān	n.	switch
4.	数值	shùzhí	n.	value
5.	断电	duàndiàn	phr.	power off
6.	短接	duǎnjiē	v.	short-circuit
7.	通电	tōngdiàn	phr.	power on
8.	绝缘垫	juéyuándiàn	n.	insulating mat
9.	绝缘电阻	juéyuán diànzǔ	phr.	insulation resistance
10.	阻值	zǔzhí	n.	resistance value
11.	绝缘性能	juéyuán xìngnéng	phr.	insulation performance

补充专业词语　Supplementary Specialized Vocabulary

1.	流程	liúchéng	n.	process, procedure
2.	正极	zhèngjí	n.	positive pole
3.	负极	fùjí	n.	negative pole
4.	空调压缩机	kōngtiáo yāsuōjī	phr.	air conditioning compressor
5.	DC/DC 转换器	DC/DC zhuǎnhuànqì	phr.	DC-to-DC converter

句子 Sentences

1. 首先进行兆欧表自检，然后检测绝缘垫，最后进行高压部件检测。
2. 用兆欧表测量绝缘垫车前、车后、车左、车右、车中 5 个点的绝缘电阻。

4

Kōngtiáo xìtǒng
空调系统
Air Conditioning System

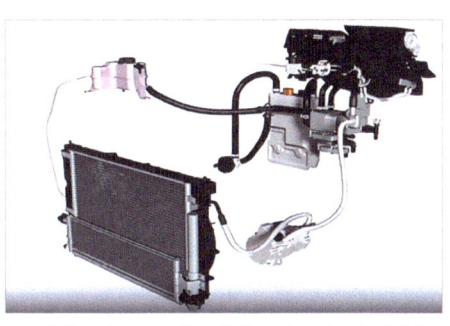

diàndòng qìchē kōngtiáo xìtǒng bāokuò zhìlěng xìtǒng、 zhìrè xìtǒng、
电动 汽车 空调 系统 包括 制冷 系统、制热 系统、
tōngfēng xìtǒng hé kōngqì jìnghuà xìtǒng děng bùfen
通风 系统和空气 净化 系统 等 部分

The air conditioning system of an electric vehicle includes the refrigeration system, heating system, ventilation system, air purification system, etc.

kōngtiáo xìtǒng
空调 系统
air conditioning system

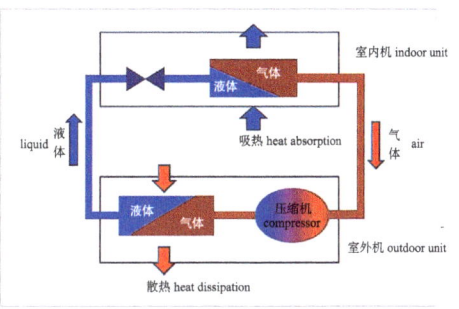

zhìlěng xìtǒng zhǔyào yóu zhēngfāqì、 yāsuōjī、 lěngníngqì、
制冷 系统主要 由 蒸发器、压缩机、冷凝器、
chǔyèguàn、 péngzhàngfá děng zǔchéng
储液罐、 膨胀阀 等 组成

The refrigeration system is mainly composed of an evaporator, a compressor, a condenser, a liquid storage tank, an expansion valve, etc.

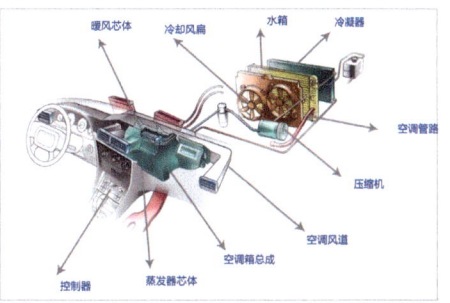

cǎinuǎn xìtǒng zhǔyào yóu gǔfēngjī、 jiārèqì、 diàndòng
采暖 系统 主要 由 鼓风机、加热器、电动
shuǐbèng、 jiārèqìxīn děng zǔchéng
水泵、 加热器芯等 组成

The heating system is mainly composed of a blower, a heater, an electric water pump, a heater core, etc.

39

题解 Introduction

1. 学习内容：电动汽车空调系统的作用和组成。
   Learning content: The functions and components of the air conditioning system of electric vehicles
2. 知识目标：掌握空调系统相关核心词汇，了解汉字的笔画 "㇏" "㇂" "㇁" "ㄟ"、笔顺 "先外后里再封口"，学写相关汉字。
   Knowledge objectives: To master the core vocabulary related to the air conditioning system, learn the strokes "㇏", "㇂", "㇁", "ㄟ" and the stroke order "outside strokes before inside strokes, and then sealing strokes" of Chinese characters, and write the related characters
3. 技能目标：熟悉空调系统的工作原理，正确使用空调制冷系统和制热系统。
   Skill objective: To be familiar with the working principle of the air conditioning system and use the refrigeration system and heating system of air conditioners correctly

第一部分　Part 1

课文　Texts

一、热身　rèshēn　Warm-up

1. 给词语选择对应的图片。Choose the corresponding pictures for the words.

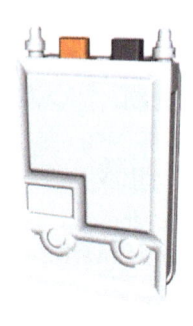

A.

B.

C.

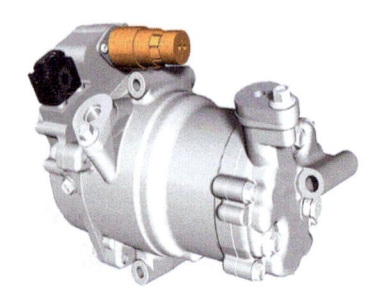

D.

空调系统 4
Air Conditioning System

　　lěngníngqì
① 冷凝器＿＿＿＿＿＿＿＿＿＿
　　condenser

　　yāsuōjī
② 压缩机＿＿＿＿＿＿＿＿＿＿
　　compressor

　　jiārèqì
③ 加热器＿＿＿＿＿＿＿＿＿＿
　　heater

　　diàndòng lěngquèyèbèng
④ 电动 冷却液泵＿＿＿＿＿＿＿＿＿＿
　　electric coolant pump

2. 看视频，认识电动汽车的空调系统，选出图中数字所代表的部件名称。**Watch the video to understand the air conditioning system of electric vehicles, and choose the names of the parts represented by the numbers in the picture.**

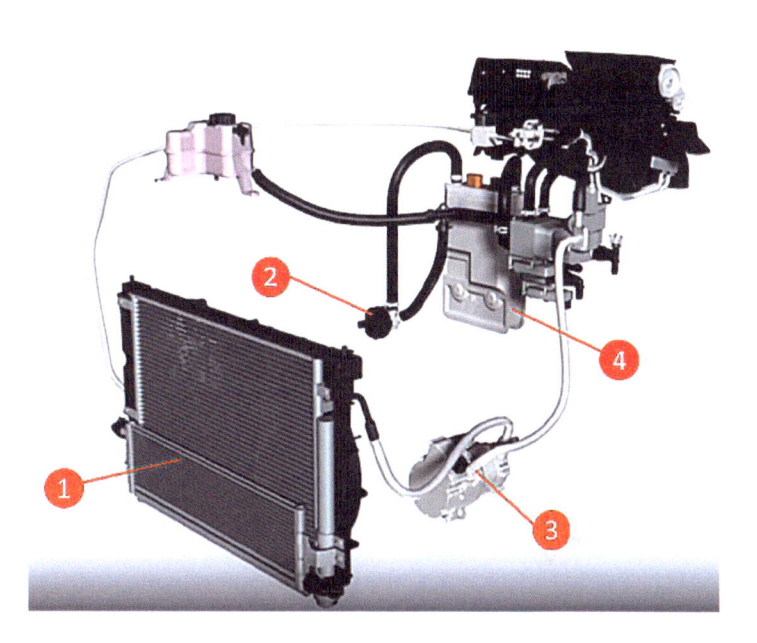

　　diàndòng lěngquèyèbèng
A. 电动 冷却液泵
　（1）＿＿＿＿＿

　　lěngníngqì
B. 冷凝器
　（2）＿＿＿＿＿

　　jiārèqì
C. 加热器
　（3）＿＿＿＿＿

　　yāsuōjī
D. 压缩机
　（4）＿＿＿＿＿

41

二、课文 kèwén Texts

A 04-01

túdi: Shīfu, tiānqì zhēn rè a!
徒弟：师傅，天气真热啊！

shīfu: Bǎ qìchē kōngtiáo xìtǒng dǎkāi, yíhuìr jiù bú rè le. Qìchē kōngtiáo xìtǒng shì duì chēxiāng nèi kōngqì jìnxíng zhìlěng、cǎinuǎn、tōngfēng hé kōngqì jìnghuà de zhuāngzhì.
师傅：把汽车空调系统打开，一会儿就不热了。汽车空调系统是对车厢内空气进行制冷、采暖、通风和空气净化的装置。

túdi: Tā yǒu shénme zuòyòng ne?
徒弟：它有什么作用呢？

shīfu: Tā wèi chéng chē rényuán tígōng shūshì de chéng chē huánjìng, jiàngdī jiàshǐ rényuán de píláo chéngdù, tígāo xíngchē ānquán.
师傅：它为乘车人员提供舒适的乘车环境，降低驾驶人员的疲劳程度，提高行车安全。

译文 yìwén Text in English

Apprentice: Master, it's so hot!

Master: Turn on the air conditioning system of the vehicle, and it will cool down soon. The automotive air conditioning system is the device for the cooling, heating, ventilation and purification of the air in the car.

Apprentice: What does it do?

Master: It provides a comfortable riding environment for passengers, reduces the level of fatigue of drivers and improves driving safety.

普通词语 pǔtōng cíyǔ General Vocabulary 04-02

1.	天气	tiānqì	n.	weather
2.	真	zhēn	adv.	truly
3.	热	rè	adj.	hot
4.	啊	a	part.	*used at the end of an exclamation for emphasis*
5.	空调	kōngtiáo	n.	air conditioning, air conditioner
6.	一会儿	yíhuìr	q.	soon
7.	空气	kōngqì	n.	air
8.	乘车人员	chéng chē rényuán	phr.	passenger
9.	舒适	shūshì	adj.	comfortable
10.	环境	huánjìng	n.	environment
11.	降低	jiàngdī	v.	reduce

12.	疲劳	píláo	adj.	tired
13.	程度	chéngdù	n.	degree, level
14.	提高	tígāo	v.	improve

专业词语 zhuānyè cíyǔ Specialized Vocabulary 🎧 04-03

1.	空调系统	kōngtiáo xìtǒng	phr.	air conditioning system
2.	车厢	chēxiāng	n.	compartment, cabin
3.	制冷	zhìlěng	v.	refrigerate cool
4.	采暖	cǎinuǎn	v.	heat
5.	通风	tōngfēng	v.	ventilate
6.	净化	jìnghuà	v.	purify
7.	装置	zhuāngzhì	n.	device
8.	行车	xíngchē	v.	drive

B 🎧 04-04

师傅： 电动汽车的空调系统分为制冷系统、采暖系统、通风系统、空气净化系统等部分。

徒弟： 师傅，各系统分别是由什么部分组成的呢？

师傅： 制冷系统主要由蒸发器、压缩机、冷凝器、储液罐、膨胀阀以及高低压管路等组成。

徒弟： 采暖系统呢？

师傅： 采暖系统主要由鼓风机、加热器、电动冷却液泵等组成。

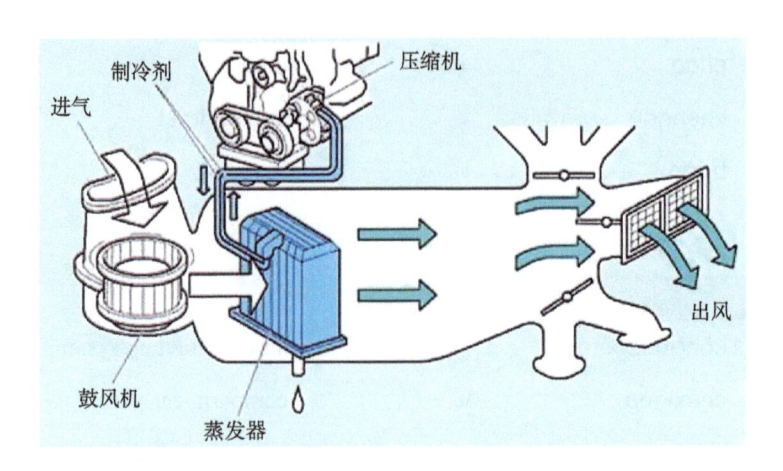

译文 yìwén Text in English

Master: The air conditioning system of an electric vehicle can be devided into the refrigeration system, the heating system, the ventilation system, the air purification system and so on.

Apprentice: Master, what is each system composed of?

Master: The refrigeration system is mainly composed of an evaporator, a compressor, a condenser, a liquid storage tank, an expansion valve, and high-pressure and low-pressure pipelines, etc.

Apprentice: What about the heating system?

Master: The heating system is mainly composed of a blower, a heater, an electric coolant pump, and a heater core, etc.

普通词语 pǔtōng cíyǔ General Vocabulary   04-05

1.	分	fēn	v.	divide
2.	以及	yǐjí	conj.	and
3.	各	gè	pron.	each
4.	分别	fēnbié	adv.	respectively

专业词语 zhuānyè cíyǔ Specialized Vocabulary   04-06

1.	制冷系统	zhìlěng xìtǒng	phr.	refrigeration system
2.	采暖系统	cǎinuǎn xìtǒng	phr.	heating system
3.	通风系统	tōngfēng xìtǒng	phr.	ventilation system
4.	空气净化系统	kōngqì jìnghuà xìtǒng	phr.	air purification system
5.	蒸发器	zhēngfāqì	n.	evaporator
6.	压缩机	yāsuōjī	n.	compressor
7.	冷凝器	lěngníngqì	n.	condenser
8.	储液罐	chǔyèguàn	n.	liquid storage tank

9.	膨胀阀	péngzhàngfá	n.	expansion valve
10.	高低压管路	gāo-dīyā guǎnlù	phr.	high-pressure and low-pressure pipelines
11.	鼓风机	gǔfēngjī	n.	blower
12.	加热器	jiārèqì	n.	heater
13.	电动冷却液泵	diàndòng lěngquèyèbèng	phr.	electric coolant pump

三、视听说 shì-tīng-shuō Viewing, Listening and Speaking

1. 观看介绍空调制冷系统工作原理的相关视频，并将制冷系统的主要部件填入正确的位置。**Watch the related video introducing the working principle of the air conditioning refrigeration system, and fill the main components of the refrigeration system in the correct positions.**

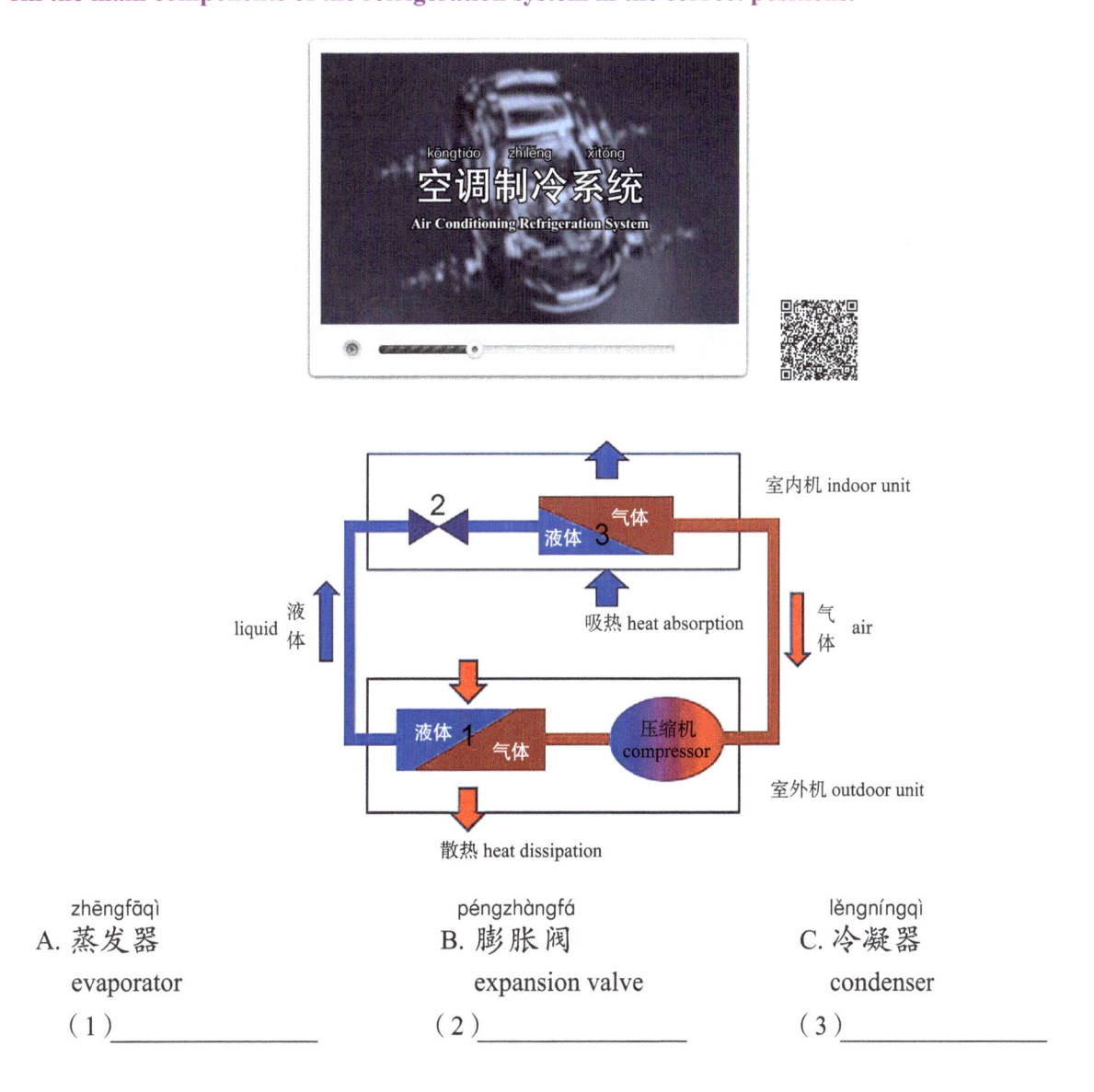

zhēngfāqì
A. 蒸发器
evaporator
（1）_____

péngzhàngfá
B. 膨胀阀
expansion valve
（2）_____

lěngníngqì
C. 冷凝器
condenser
（3）_____

2. 请试着说出电动汽车空调制冷系统的工作原理。**Please try to explain the working principle of the air conditioning refrigeration system of electric vehicles.**

四、学以致用　xuéyǐzhìyòng　Practicing What You Have Learnt

观看介绍空调采暖系统工作原理的相关视频，并将采暖系统的主要部件填入正确的位置。Watch the related video introducing the working principle of air conditioning heating system, and fill the main components of heating system in the correct positions.

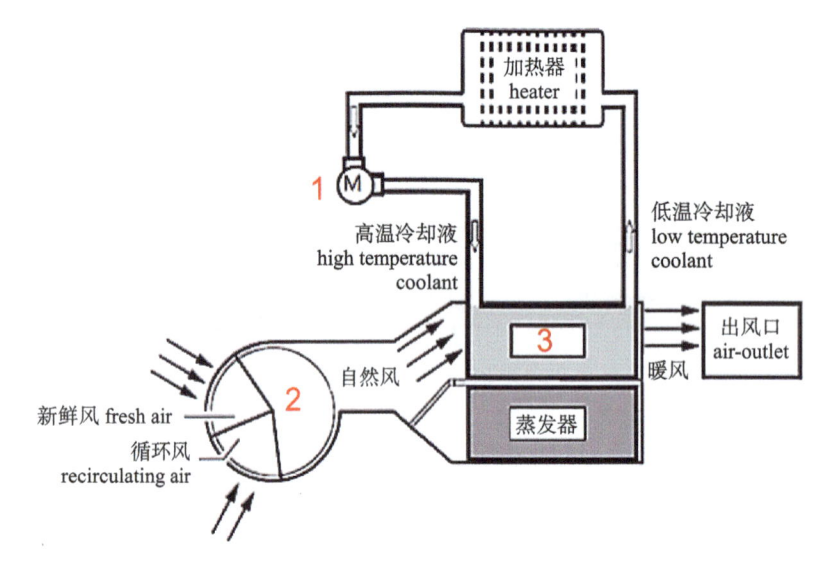

kōngtiáo　cǎinuǎn　xìtǒng
空调采暖系统
Air Conditioning Heating System

加热器 heater
高温冷却液 high temperature coolant
低温冷却液 low temperature coolant
出风口 air-outlet
暖风
蒸发器
自然风
新鲜风 fresh air
循环风 recirculating air

　　gǔfēngjī　　　　　　　　　jiārèqìxīn　　　　　　　　diàndòng lěngquèyèbèng
A. 鼓风机　　　　　　　　B. 加热器芯　　　　　　C. 电动冷却液泵
　　blower　　　　　　　　　heater core　　　　　　electric coolant pump

（1）_____　　　（2）_____　　　（3）_____

五、小知识　xiǎozhīshi　Tips

Wēndù shèdìng bùyí guò dī
温度设定不宜过低

　　Zài tiānqì bǐjiào yánrè de shíhou,　　hěn duō rén dōu xǐhuan bǎ wēndù shèdìng de fēicháng dī,
在天气比较炎热的时候，很多人都喜欢把温度设定得非常低，
ràng chē nèi bǎochí shífēn liángshuǎng de wēndù,　yǔ wàimiàn de yányán lièrì xíngchéng "bīng huǒ
让 车内保持十分 凉爽 的温度，与外面的炎炎烈日形成"冰火

46

liǎng chóng tiān". Wēndù shèdìng de guò dī, huì zēngjiā dònglì xùdiànchízǔ de fùdān, zàochéng
两 重 天"。温度设定得过低,会增加动力蓄电池组的负担,造成
dònglì xiàjiàng yǔ hàodiànliàng shàngshēng. Chē nèi chē wài wēnchā tài dà, hái huì ràng réntǐ chǎn-
动力下降与耗电量 上升。车内车外温差太大,还会让人体产
shēng búshì, shènzhì yǐnqǐ gǎnmào, duì jiànkāng búlì.
生 不适,甚至引起 感冒,对健康不利。

The Temperature Should Not Be Set Too Low

On hot days, many people like to set the temperature very low to keep a pleasantly cool temperature inside the vehicle, in stark contrast to the scorching sun outside. If the temperature is set too low, it will increase the burden on the power storage battery pack, resulting in a decline in power and an increase in power consumption. If the temperature difference between the inside and outside of the vehicle is too large, people will feel uncomfortable and even catch a cold, which is bad for people's health.

补充专业词语 bǔchōng zhuānyè cíyǔ Supplementary Specialized Vocabulary 🎧 04-07

1.	设定	shèdìng	v.	set
2.	动力蓄电池组	dònglì xùdiànchízǔ	phr.	power storage battery pack
3.	负担	fùdān	n.	burden
4.	耗电量	hàodiànliàng	n.	power consumption
5.	温差	wēnchā	n.	temperature difference

第二部分 Part 2   汉字 Chinese Characters

一、汉字知识 Hànzì zhīshi Knowledge about Chinese Characters

1. 汉字的笔画(4) Strokes of Chinese characters (4)

笔画 Strokes	名称 Names	例字 Examples
㇀	提 tí	习
㇊	竖提 shùtí	衣
㇆	横折提 héngzhétí	语
㇇	撇点 piědiǎn	女

2. 汉字的笔顺(4) Stroke orders of Chinese characters (4)

规则 Rule	例字 Examples	笔顺 Stroke orders
先外后里再封口 Outside strokes before inside strokes, and then sealing strokes	国 日	丨冂冂同同国国国 丨冂冂日

二、汉字认读与书写　　Hànzì rèndú yǔ shūxiě　　The Recognition and Writing of Chinese Characters

认读下列词语，并试着读写构成词语的汉字。
Recognize the following words, and try to read and write the Chinese characters forming these words.

提高　　以及　　换气　　装置

提		高		以		及	
换		气		装		置	

第三部分　Part 3　日常用语 Daily Expressions

❶ 我们机场见。Wǒmen jīchǎng jiàn. See you at the airport.

❷ 我们电话（邮件）联系。Wǒmen diànhuà (yóujiàn) liánxì. Let's contact by phone/e-mail.

❸ 下星期一到北京的航班还有票吗？　Xià xīngqīyī dào Běijīng de hángbān hái yǒu piào ma?
Are there any tickets available for next Monday's flight to Beijing?

第四部分　Part 4　单元实训 Unit Practical Training

正确使用空调系统
Proper Use of Air Conditioning System

实训目的 Training purpose

通过实训，实训人员能够熟悉汽车空调系统的工作原理，并正确使用空调制冷系统和采暖系统。
Through the practical training, the trainees are able to familiarize themselves with the working principle of the air conditioning system of electric vehicles and use the air conditioning refrigeration system and heating system correctly.

实训组织 Training organization

每组 4 人
four trainees in each group

实训步骤 Training steps

❶ 教师准备一台电动汽车。
　　The teacher prepares an electric vehicle.

❷ 学员分组，每组 4 人。
　　Divide the trainees into groups of 4.

48

❸ 学员正确操作空调系统并说出工作流程。

The trainees operate the air conditioning system correctly and explain the working process.

❹ 学员互评。

The trainees carry out peer assessment.

❺ 教师总结评价，实训结束。

The teacher summarizes and evaluates, and the training ends.

第五部分　Part 5　单元小结　Unit Summary

词语 cíyǔ Vocabulary

普通词语　General Vocabulary

1.	天气	tiānqì	n.	weather
2.	真	zhēn	adv.	truly
3.	热	rè	adj.	hot
4.	啊	a	part.	used at the end of an exclamation for emphasis
5.	空调	kōngtiáo	n.	air conditioning, air conditioner
6.	一会儿	yíhuìr	q.	soon
7.	空气	kōngqì	n.	air
8.	乘车人员	chéng chē rényuán	phr.	passenger
9.	舒适	shūshì	adj.	comfortable
10.	环境	huánjìng	n.	environment
11.	降低	jiàngdī	v.	reduce
12.	疲劳	píláo	adj.	tired
13.	程度	chéngdù	n.	degree, level
14.	提高	tígāo	v.	improve
15.	分	fēn	v.	divide
16.	以及	yǐjí	conj.	and
17.	各	gè	pron.	each
18.	分别	fēnbié	adv.	respectively

专业词语　Specialized Vocabulary

1.	空调系统	kōngtiáo xìtǒng	phr.	air conditioning system
2.	车厢	chēxiāng	n.	compartment, cabin
3.	制冷	zhìlěng	v.	refrigerate, cool

cíyǔ 词语 Vocabulary

4.	采暖	cǎinuǎn	v.	heat
5.	通风	tōngfēng	v.	ventilate
6.	净化	jìnghuà	v.	purify
7.	装置	zhuāngzhì	n.	device
8.	行车	xíngchē	v.	drive
9.	制冷系统	zhìlěng xìtǒng	phr.	refrigeration system
10.	采暖系统	cǎinuǎn xìtǒng	phr.	heating system
11.	通风系统	tōngfēng xìtǒng	phr.	ventilation system
12.	空气净化系统	kōngqì jìnghuà xìtǒng	phr.	air purification system
13.	蒸发器	zhēngfāqì	n.	evaporator
14.	压缩机	yāsuōjī	n.	compressor
15.	冷凝器	lěngníngqì	n.	condenser
16.	储液罐	chǔyèguàn	n.	liquid storage tank
17.	膨胀阀	péngzhàngfá	n.	expansion valve
18.	高低压管路	gāo-dīyā guǎnlù	phr.	high-pressure and low-pressure pipelines
19.	鼓风机	gǔfēngjī	n.	blower
20.	加热器	jiārèqì	n.	heater
21.	电动冷却液泵	diàndòng lěngquèyèbèng	phr.	electric coolant pump

补充专业词语 Supplementary Specialized Vocabulary

1.	设定	shèdìng	v.	set
2.	动力蓄电池组	dònglì xùdiànchízǔ	phr.	power storage battery pack
3.	负担	fùdān	n.	burden
4.	耗电量	hàodiànliàng	n.	power consumption
5.	温差	wēnchā	n.	temperature difference

jùzi 句子 Sentences

1. 汽车空调系统是对车厢内空气进行制冷、采暖、通风和空气净化的装置。
2. 制冷系统主要由蒸发器、压缩机、冷凝器、储液罐、膨胀阀以及高低压管路等组成。
3. 采暖系统主要由鼓风机、加热器、电动冷却液泵等组成。

5

Diǎnxíng chuángǎnqì
典型传感器
Typical Sensors

diǎnxíng chuángǎnqì
典型 传感器
typical sensors

- **xuánbiàn chuángǎnqì**
  旋变 传感器
  resolver

- **wēndù chuángǎnqì**
  温度 传感器
  temperature sensor

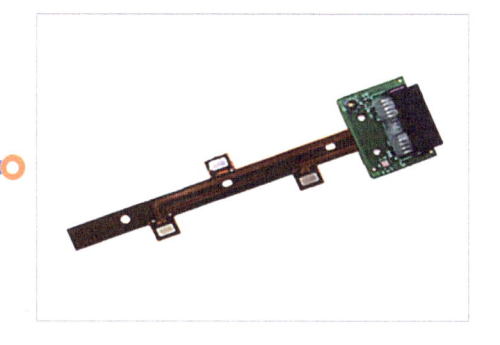

- **diànchí zhìnéng chuángǎnqì**
  电池 智能 传感器
  battery smart sensor

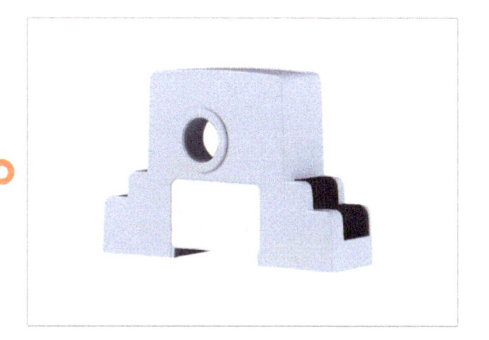

- **diànliú chuángǎnqì**
  电流 传感器
  current sensor

51

> **题解　Introduction**
>
> 1. 学习内容：电动汽车典型传感器的特点。
>   Learning content: The characteristics of typical sensors of electric vehicles
> 2. 知识目标：掌握电动汽车典型传感器的核心词汇，了解汉字的笔画"㇏""㇙""亅""乙"和独体结构，学写相关汉字。
>   Knowledge objectives: To master the core vocabulary related to the typical sensors of electric vehicles, learn the strokes "㇏", "㇙", "亅", "乙" and the independent structure of Chinese characters, and write the related characters
> 3. 技能目标：了解旋变传感器、温度传感器、电流传感器和电池智能传感器的位置、作用和特点，掌握传感器检测。
>   Skill objective: To learn about the positions, functions and characteristics of resolvers, temperature sensors, current sensors and battery smart sensors, and master the testing of sensors

第一部分　Part 1

课文　Texts

一、热身　rèshēn　Warm-up

1. 给词语选择对应的图片。Choose the corresponding pictures for the words.

A.

B.

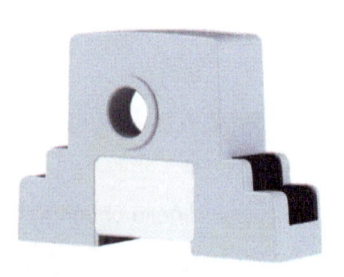

C.

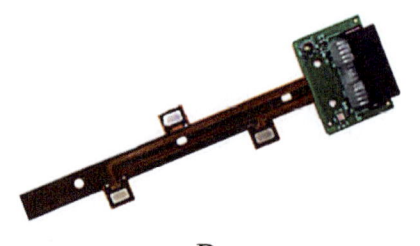

D.

❶ wēndù chuánggǎnqì
温度 传感器 ＿＿＿＿＿＿
temperature sensor

❷ xuánbiàn chuánggǎnqì
旋变 传感器 ＿＿＿＿＿＿
resolver

典型传感器 5
Typical Sensors

    zhìnéng chuánggǎnqì
❸ 智能 传感器_____
    smart sensor

    diànliú chuánggǎnqì
❹ 电流 传感器_____
    current sensor

2. 看视频，了解不同传感器的安装位置，将下列传感器的图片与其所在的汽车零件配对。Watch the video to learn about the installation positions of different sensors, and match the following pictures of the sensors with the vehicle parts they are in.

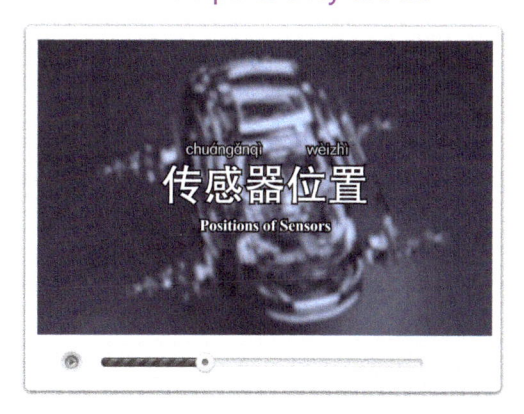

A 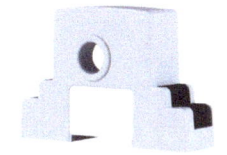   B    C    D

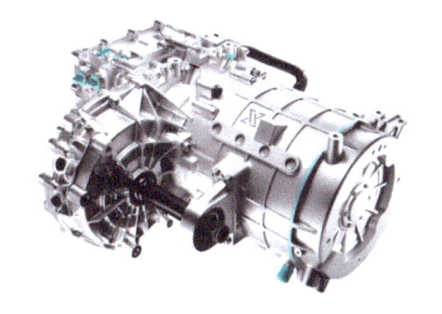

qūdòng diànjī
驱动 电机
driving motor

duìyìng chuánggǎnqì:
对应 传感器：
corresponding sensors: _____

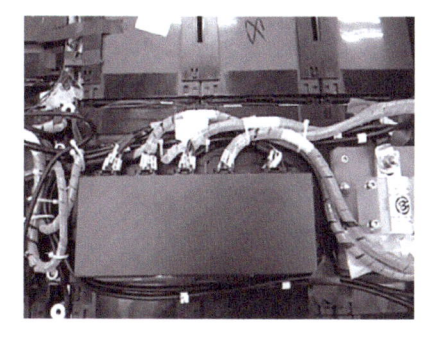

diànchí guǎnlǐ xìtǒng
电池 管理 系统
battery management system

duìyìng chuánggǎnqì:
对应 传感器：
corresponding sensors: _____

53

三、课文 kèwén Texts

A 05-01

jīdiàn wéixiūgōng: Zhè tái diàndòng qìchē yǒudiǎnr wèntí, kěnéng shì chuángǎnqì chū gùzhàng le.
机电 维修工：这台电动汽车有点儿问题，可能是传感器出故障了。

jìshù zǒngjiān: Nǎge chuángǎnqì chū wèntí le? Nǐ jiǎnchále méiyǒu?
技术 总监：哪个传感器出问题了？你检查了没有？

jīdiàn wéixiūgōng: Hái méiyǒu.
机电 维修工：还没有。

jìshù zǒngjiān: Nǐ cóng jǐ gè diǎnxíng chuángǎnqì kāishǐ zhěnduàn, bāokuò xuánbiàn chuángǎnqì、wēndù chuángǎnqì、diànliú chuángǎnqì hé diànchí zhìnéng chuángǎnqì.
技术 总监：你从几个典型传感器开始诊断，包括 旋变 传感器、温度传感器、电流 传感器和电池 智能 传感器。

jīdiàn wéixiūgōng: Bù tóng chuángǎnqì fēnbié jiǎncè shénme?
机电 维修工：不同 传感器 分别检测什么？

jìshù zǒngjiān: Xuánbiàn chuángǎnqì jiǎncè wèizhì, wēndù chuángǎnqì jiǎncè wēndù, diànliú chuángǎnqì jiǎncè diànliú, diànchí zhìnéng chuángǎnqì jiǎncè diànliú、diànyā hé wēndù.
技术 总监：旋变 传感器 检测位置，温度传感器检测温度，电流 传感器 检测电流，电池 智能 传感器 检测电流、电压和温度。

译文 yìwén Text in English

Mechanical and Electrical Maintenance Technician: There is something wrong with this electric vehicle. Maybe the sensor is out of order.

Technical Director: Which sensor is out of order? Have you checked?

Mechanical and Electrical Maintenance Technician: Not yet.

Technical Director: You start the diagnosis with several typical sensors, including the resolver, temperature sensor, current sensor, and battery smart sensor.

Mechanical and Electrical Maintenance Technician: What do different sensors detect?

Technical Director: The resolver detects location, the temperature sensor detects temperature, the current sensor detects current, and the battery smart sensor detects current, voltage and temperature.

普通词语 pǔtōng cíyǔ General Vocabulary 05-02

1.	台	tái	m.	used for certain machines, apparatuses, etc.
2.	问题	wèntí	n.	problem
3.	可能	kěnéng	v.	maybe, perhaps

4.	典型	diǎnxíng	adj.	typical
5.	位置	wèizhì	n.	position, location
6.	温度	wēndù	n.	temperature

专业词语 zhuānyè cíyǔ Specialized Vocabulary 🎧 05-03

1.	机电维修工	jīdiàn wéixiūgōng	phr.	mechanical and electrical maintenance technician
2.	技术总监	jìshù zǒngjiān	phr.	technical director
3.	传感器	chuángǎnqì	n.	sensor
4.	旋变传感器	xuánbiàn chuángǎnqì	phr.	resolver
5.	温度传感器	wēndù chuángǎnqì	phr.	temperature sensor
6.	电流传感器	diànliú chuángǎnqì	phr.	current sensor
7.	电池智能传感器	diànchí zhìnéng chuángǎnqì	phr.	battery smart sensor

B 🎧 05-04

徒弟：师傅，刚才您讲的那几种传感器都安装在哪儿？

师傅：旋变传感器、温度传感器和电流传感器安装在驱动电机中。电池智能传感器安装在电池管理系统中。

徒弟：驱动电机中的传感器安装在什么位置？

师傅：电流传感器通常安装在电机内部，温度传感器安装在驱动电机的后端盖上或者定子上，旋变传感器安装在转子上。

徒弟：驱动电机中的传感器检测哪些信息？

师傅：电流传感器用来检测电机的电流。温度传感器用来检测驱动电机的温度，避免温度过高造成组件损坏。

译文 yìwén Text in English

Apprentice: Master, where are the sensors you just mentioned installed?

Master: The resolver, temperature sensor and current sensor are installed in the driving motor. The battery smart sensor is installed in the battery management system.

Apprentice: Where are the sensors in the driving motor installed?

Master: The current sensor is usually installed inside the motor, the temperature sensor is installed on the rear end cover or on the stator of the driving motor, and the resolver is installed on the rotor.

Apprentice: What information is detected by the sensors in the driving motor?

Master: The current sensor is used to detect the current of the motor. The temperature sensor is used to detect the temperature of the driving motor, to avoid component damage due to excessive temperature.

普通词语 pǔtōng cíyǔ General Vocabulary 🎧 05-05

1.	刚才	gāngcái	n.	the time just past
2.	几	jǐ	pron.	several
3.	内部	nèibù	n.	inside
4.	避免	bìmiǎn	v.	avoid
5.	过	guò	adv.	excessively, too
6.	造成	zàochéng	v.	cause
7.	损坏	sǔnhuài	v.	damage

专业词语 zhuānyè cíyǔ Specialized Vocabulary 🎧 05-06

1.	后端盖	hòuduāngài	n.	rear end cover
2.	定子	dìngzǐ	n.	stator
3.	转子	zhuànzǐ	n.	rotor
4.	组件	zǔjiàn	n.	component

三、视听说 shì-tīng-shuō Viewing, Listening and Speaking

观看介绍电动汽车传感器作用的相关视频，将各传感器与其检测的信号进行连线，并说出不同传感器的特点。**Watch the related video introducing the functions of electric vehicle sensors, connect different sensors to the signals they detect, and name the characteristics of different sensors.**

传感器作用
chuángǎnqì zuòyòng
Functions of Sensors

典型传感器 5
Typical Sensors

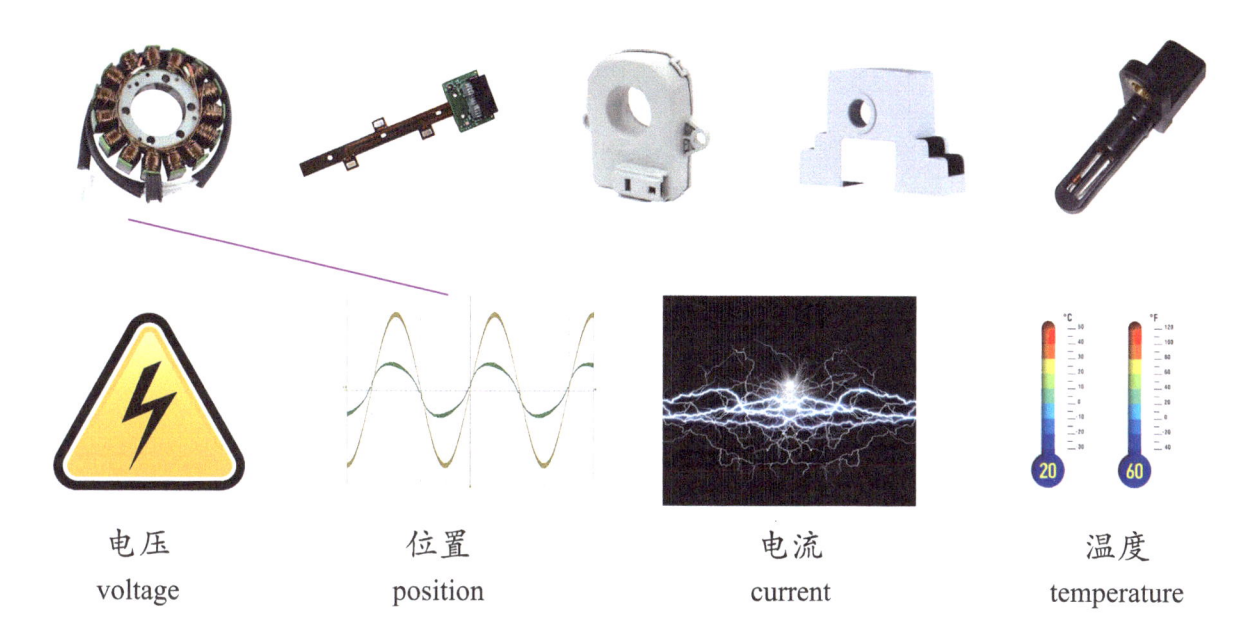

电压
voltage

位置
position

电流
current

温度
temperature

四、学以致用　xuéyǐzhìyòng　**Practicing What You Have Learnt**

观看介绍温度、旋变传感器的相关视频，指出温度传感器和旋变传感器的位置。**Watch the related video introducing the temperature sensor and the resolver, and point out their locations.**

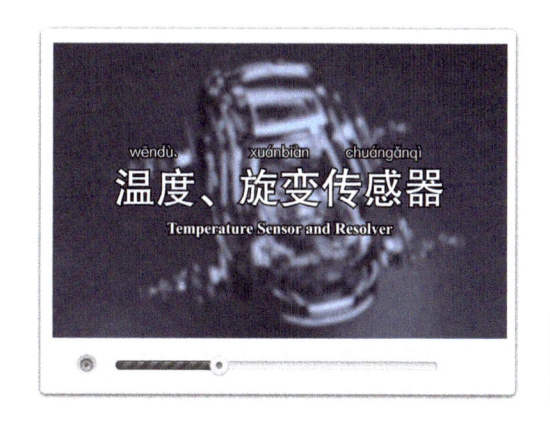

Wēndù chuángǎnqì zài　　　　　　shang, xuánbiàn chuángǎnqì zài　　　　　　shang.
温度 传感器 在（1）＿＿＿＿＿＿上，旋变 传感器 在（2）＿＿＿＿＿＿上。
The temperature sensor is on (1)＿＿＿＿＿＿, and the resolver is on (2)＿＿＿＿＿＿.

57

五、小知识　xiǎozhīshi　Tips

典型传感器的位置与作用

1. 旋变传感器安装在驱动电机的定子上，使用电压信号确定转子相对于定子的位置，从而切换定子的电流方向。

2. 温度传感器安装在驱动电机端盖上，用来检测驱动电机的温度，避免温度过高造成组件损坏。

3. 电流传感器安装在驱动电机中，用以检测电机工作的实际电流。电流传感器也安装在电池管理系统中，用来检测充放电电流的大小。

4. 智能电池传感器用来监控电池的电压、电流、温度等信息，通过电池管理系统，保障串联电池的性能一致性。

Locations and Functions of Typical Sensors

1. The resolver is installed on the stator of the driving motor, using the voltage signal to determine the position of the rotor relative to the stator, thereby switching the current direction of the stator.

2. The temperature sensor is installed on the end cover of the driving motor to monitor the temperature of the driving motor to avoid component damage due to excessive temperature.

3. The current sensor is installed inside the driving motor to detect the actual operating current of the motor. The current sensor is also installed in the battery management system to detect the magnitude of the charging and discharging current.

4. The battery smart sensor is used to monitor the voltage, current, temperature and other information of the battery, to guarantee the consistency of performance of the series battery through the battery management system.

补充专业词语 bǔchōng zhuānyè cíyǔ Supplementary Specialized Vocabulary 🎧 05-07

1.	充放电	chōng-fàngdiàn	v.	charge and discharge
2.	串联电池	chuànlián diànchí	phr.	series battery

第二部分 Part 2 汉字 Chinese Characters

一、汉字知识 Hànzì zhīshi Knowledge about Chinese Characters

1. 汉字的笔画（5） **Strokes of Chinese characters (5)**

笔画 Strokes	名称 Names	例字 Examples
㇂	斜钩 xiégōu	我
㇁	卧钩 wògōu	心
𠃌	横折钩 héngzhégōu	问
乙	横折弯钩 héngzhéwāngōu	几

2. 汉字的结构（1） **Structures of Chinese characters (1)**

结构类型 Structure type	例字 Examples	结构图示 Illustration
独体结构 Independent structure	生 不	□

二、汉字认读与书写 Hànzì rèndú yǔ shūxiě The Recognition and Writing of Chinese Characters

认读下列词语，并试着读写构成词语的汉字。
Recognize the following words, and try to read and write the Chinese characters forming these words.

传感器　温度　电流　智能

传			感			器			
温			度			电			流
智			能						

第三部分 Part 3 日常用语 Daily Expressions

❶ 我要两张 11 号到上海的火车票。Wǒ yào liǎng zhāng 11 hào dào Shànghǎi de huǒchēpiào.
I want two train tickets to Shanghai on the 11th.

❷ 我的护照和钱包都丢了。Wǒ de hùzhào hé qiánbāo dōu diū le. I've lost both my passport and purse.

❸ 还可以便宜一些吗？ Hái kěyǐ piányi yìxiē ma? Can you give me this for a cheaper price?

第四部分 Part 4 单元实训 Unit Practical Training

温度传感器检测
Testing of Temperature Sensors

实训目的 Training purpose

通过实训，实训人员能够掌握温度传感器是否正常的检测方法。

Through the practical training, the trainees are able to master the methods of testing whether the temperature sensor is normal.

实训组织 Training organization

每组 4 人

four trainees in each group

实训步骤 Training steps

❶ 教师带领学员围绕在拆解了的驱动电机周围，查找温度传感器的位置。

The teacher leads the trainees around the disassembled driving motor to find the location of the temperature sensor.

❷ 每组学员讨论确定所需的检测工具。

Each group of trainees discuss and determine the required testing tools.

❸ 教师进行演示操作：

The teacher conducts a demonstration operation:

- 用电阻表分别连接温度传感器接线端子；
- Connect the terminals of the temperature sensor with a resistance meter;
- 查看电阻表显示的电阻值是否在 50.04～212.5kΩ 范围内；
- Check whether the resistance value displayed by the resistance meter is within the range of 50.04～212.5kΩ.
- 如果电阻不在范围内，则异常。
- If the resistance is not within the range, it is abnormal.

❹ 学员进行练习。

The trainees practice.

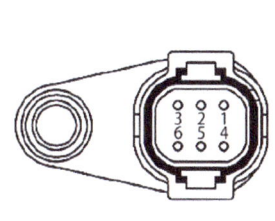

端子号	定义
1	
2	
3	温度传感器：红+
4	
5	
6	温度传感器：黑-

第五部分　Part 5

单元小结　Unit Summary

词语 cíyǔ Vocabulary

普通词语　General Vocabulary

1.	台	tái	m.	*used for certain machines, apparatuses, etc.*
2.	问题	wèntí	n.	problem
3.	可能	kěnéng	v.	maybe, perhaps
4.	典型	diǎnxíng	adj.	typical
5.	位置	wèizhì	n.	position, location
6.	温度	wēndù	n.	temperature
7.	刚才	gāngcái	n.	the time just past
8.	几	jǐ	pron.	several
9.	内部	nèibù	n.	inside
10.	避免	bìmiǎn	v.	avoid
11.	过	guò	adv.	excessively, too
12.	造成	zàochéng	v.	cause
13.	损坏	sǔnhuài	v.	damage

专业词语　Specialized Vocabulary

1.	机电维修工	jīdiàn wéixiūgōng	phr.	mechanical and electrical maintenance technician
2.	技术总监	jìshù zǒngjiān	phr.	technical director
3.	传感器	chuángǎnqì	n.	sensor
4.	旋变传感器	xuánbiàn chuángǎnqì	phr.	resolver
5.	温度传感器	wēndù chuángǎnqì	phr.	temperature sensor
6.	电流传感器	diànliú chuángǎnqì	phr.	current sensor

cíyǔ **词语** Vocabulary	7.	电池智能传感器	diànchí zhìnéng chuángǎnqì	phr.	battery smart sensor
	8.	后端盖	hòuduāngài	n.	rear end cover
	9.	定子	dìngzǐ	n.	stator
	10.	转子	zhuànzǐ	n.	rotor
	11.	组件	zǔjiàn	n.	component

补充专业词语　Supplementary Specialized Vocabulary

	1.	充放电	chōngfàngdiàn	v.	charge and discharge
	2.	串联电池	chuànlián diànchí	phr.	series battery

jùzi
句子
Sentences

1. 旋变传感器检测位置，温度传感器检测温度，电流传感器检测电流，电池智能传感器检测电流、电压和温度。
2. 旋变传感器、温度传感器和电流传感器安装在驱动电机中。电池智能传感器安装在电池管理系统中。
3. 电流传感器用来检测电机工作的电流，温度传感器用来检测驱动电机温度，避免温度过高造成组件损坏。

6

Diànlùtú shídú
电路图识读
Interpretation of Circuit Diagrams

diànlùtú jiědú
电路图解读
interpretation of circuit diagrams

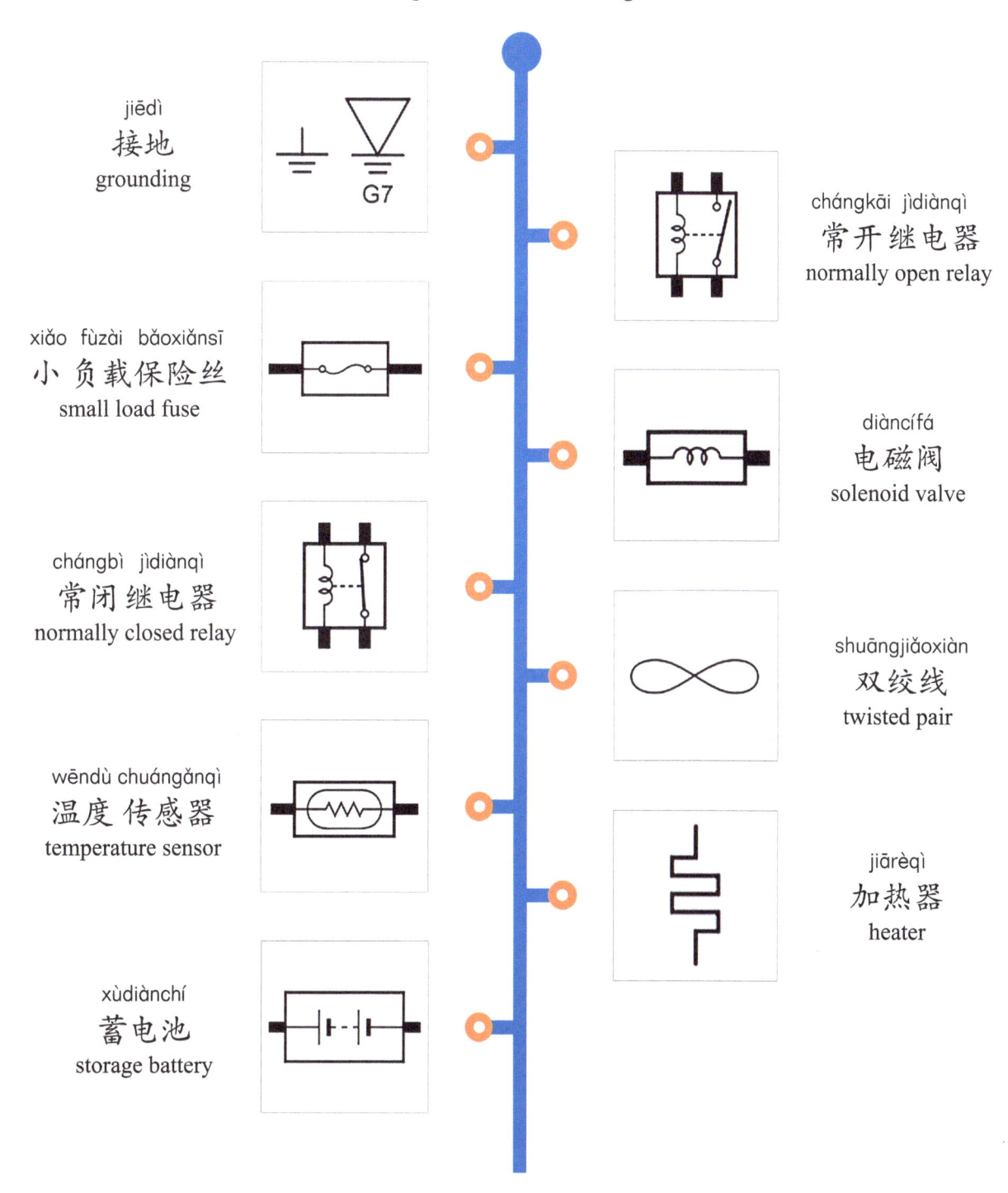

jiēdì
接地
grounding

xiǎo fùzài bǎoxiǎnsī
小 负载保险丝
small load fuse

chángbì jìdiànqì
常闭继电器
normally closed relay

wēndù chuángǎnqì
温度 传感器
temperature sensor

xùdiànchí
蓄电池
storage battery

chángkāi jìdiànqì
常开继电器
normally open relay

diàncífá
电磁阀
solenoid valve

shuāngjiǎoxiàn
双绞线
twisted pair

jiārèqì
加热器
heater

63

> **题解　Introduction**
>
> 1. 学习内容：电动汽车电路图的特点和识图方法。
>   Learning content: The characteristics and recognition method of circuit diagrams of electric vehicles
> 2. 知识目标：掌握电路图相关核心词汇，了解汉字的笔画"ʓ""ʒ"和品字形结构，学写相关汉字。
>   Knowledge objectives: To master the core vocabulary related to circuit diagrams, learn the strokes "ʓ", "ʒ" and the 品-shaped structure of Chinese characters, and write the related characters
> 3. 技能目标：了解电路图特点和识图方法，掌握解读电路图中符号和缩写的含义。
>   Skill objective: To learn about the characteristics and recognition method of circuit diagrams, and master the interpretation of the meaning of the symbols and abbreviations in circuit diagrams

第一部分　Part 1

课文　Texts

一、热身　rèshēn　Warm-up

1. 将颜色代码与相应颜色的导线连线。Connect the color codes to the leads of the corresponding colors.

R	黑色
Y	灰色
Bl	棕色
O	蓝色
B	绿色
G	红色
Gr	黄色
Br	橙色
V	白色
W	紫色
Lg	粉色
L	浅绿色
P	浅蓝色

电路图识读 6
Interpretation of Circuit Diagrams

2. 观看介绍电路图的相关视频，了解汽车电路图上的图形所代表的意思，将下列图形和其所表示的意思进行配对。**Watch the related video introducing circuit diagrams, understand the meaning of the figures in the circuit diagram of a vehicle, and match the following figures with their meanings.**

  xùdiànchí
A. 蓄电池
 storage battery

  jiēdì
B. 接地
 grounding

  chángkāi jìdiànqì
C. 常开继电器
 normally open relay

  jiārèqì
D. 加热器
 heater

  xiǎo fùzài bǎoxiǎnsī
E. 小负载保险丝
 small load fuse

  chángbì jìdiànqì
F. 常闭继电器
 normally closed relay

  shuāngjiǎoxiàn
G. 双绞线
 twisted pair

  wēndù chuángǎnqì
H. 温度传感器
 temperature sensor

  diàncífá
I. 电磁阀
 solenoid valve

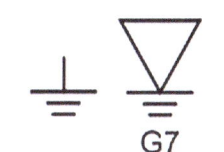

（1）_____ 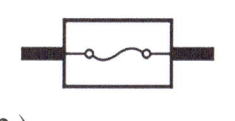 （2）_____ 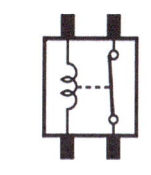 （3）_____

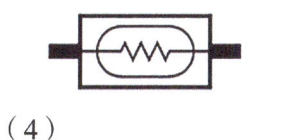

（4）_____ 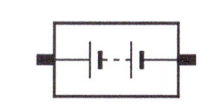 （5）_____ 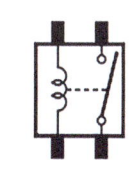 （6）_____

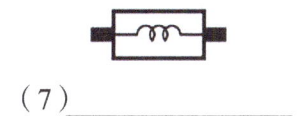

（7）_____  （8）_____ （9）_____

二、课文　kèwén　Texts

A　06-01

徒弟：师傅，这是电动汽车电路图吗？

师傅：是的，电路图将整个汽车的电路按照关联清晰地展示出来。汽车电路图具有单线制、负极接地、用电设备并联等特点。

徒弟：那您给我讲一讲这一款汽车的电路图吧。汽车电路图上的电气元件与实际位置是一一对应的吗？

师傅：并不是，汽车电路图上的电气元件依据工作原理，在图中合理布局。例如，这条黑线旁边的字母"B"是BLACK的简写，代表这条导线在车上是黑色的。

徒弟：那"G"是不是GREEN的简写，代表绿色的导线？

师傅：是的。

译文 yìwén Text in English

Apprentice: Master, is this a circuit diagram of an electric vehicle?

Master: Yes, the circuit diagram displays the whole vehicle's circuit clearly in relation to each other. The circuit diagram of a vehicle has the characteristics of single-wire system, negative grounding, electrical equipment in parallel, etc.

Apprentice: Please tell me about the circuit diagram of this vehicle. Do the electrical components in the circuit diagram of the vehicle correspond to the actual positions one-to-one?

Master: No, the electrical components in the circuit diagram of the vehicle are reasonably laid out in the diagram based on the working principle. For example, the letter "B" next to this black line is short for BLACK, which means that this lead is black in the vehicle.

Apprentice: Is "G" short for GREEN, representing a green lead?

Master: Yes, it is.

6 Interpretation of Circuit Diagrams

普通词语 pǔtōng cíyǔ General Vocabulary 🎧 06-02

1.	整个	zhěnggè	adj.	whole
2.	按照	ànzhào	prep.	according to
3.	清晰	qīngxī	adj.	clear
4.	展示	zhǎnshì	v.	display, demonstrate
5.	款	kuǎn	m.	kind
6.	实际	shíjì	adj.	actual
7.	对应	duìyìng	v.	match
8.	并	bìng	adv.	used before a negative for emphasis, usually as a retort
9.	依据	yījù	prep.	according to
10.	原理	yuánlǐ	n.	principle
11.	合理	hélǐ	adj.	reasonable
12.	布局	bùjú	v.	make overall arrangements, lay out
13.	旁边	pángbiān	n.	side
14.	简写	jiǎnxiě	n.	abbreviation
15.	代表	dàibiǎo	v.	represent
16.	黑色	hēisè	n.	black

专业词语 zhuānyè cíyǔ Specialized Vocabulary 🎧 06-03

1.	电路图	diànlùtú	n.	circuit diagram
2.	关联	guānlián	v.	be linked
3.	单线制	dānxiànzhì	n.	single-wire system
4.	接地	jiēdì	v.	ground
5.	设备	shèbèi	n.	equipment
6.	并联	bìnglián	v.	make a parallel connection
7.	电气元件	diànqì yuánjiàn	phr.	electrical component
8.	导线	dǎoxiàn	n.	lead

B 🎧 06-04

túdi: Qìchē diànlùtú shang de zhèxiē zìmǔ suōxiě biǎoshì shénme yìsi?
徒弟：汽车电路图上的这些字母缩写表示什么意思？

师傅："CA"表示发动机舱线束，"BV"代表动力线束，"IP"代表仪表线束，"SO"代表底板线束，"DR"代表门线束，"RF"代表顶棚线束。

徒弟：那这些图形分别表示什么意思呢？

师傅：这些图形分别表示接地、小负载保险丝、常闭继电器、温度传感器、蓄电池、常开继电器、电磁阀、加热器。你记住了吗？

译文 yìwén Text in English

Apprentice: What do these abbreviations on the circuit diagram of a vehicle mean?

Master: "CA" means engine compartment wiring harness. "BV" stands for power wiring harness. "IP" stands for instrument panel wiring harness. "SO" stands for chassis base wiring harness, "DR" stands for door wiring harness, and "RF" stands for roof wiring harness.

Apprentice: Then what do these figures mean respectively?

Master: These figures stand for grounding, small load fuse, normally closed relay, temperature sensor, storage battery, normally open relay, solenoid valve and heater respectively. Do you remember?

普通词语 pǔtōng cíyǔ General Vocabulary 06-05

1.	这些	zhèxiē	pron.	these
2.	字母	zìmǔ	n.	letter
3.	缩写	suōxiě	n.	abbreviation
4.	表示	biǎoshì	v.	represent, mean
5.	意思	yìsi	n.	meaning
6.	图形	túxíng	n.	graph, figure

专业词语 zhuānyè cíyǔ Specialized Vocabulary 06-06

1.	发动机舱线束	fādòngjīcāng xiànshù	phr.	engine compartment wiring harness

2.	动力线束	dònglì xiànshù	phr.	power wiring harness
3.	仪表线束	yíbiǎo xiànshù	phr.	instrument panel wiring harness
4.	底板线束	dǐbǎn xiànshù	phr.	chassis base wiring harness
5.	门线束	mén xiànshù	phr.	door wiring harness
6.	顶棚线束	dǐngpéng xiànshù	phr.	roof wiring harness
7.	小负载保险丝	xiǎo fùzài bǎoxiǎnsī	phr.	small load fuse
8.	常闭继电器	chángbì jìdiànqì	phr.	normally closed relay
9.	常开继电器	chángkāi jìdiànqì	phr.	normally open relay
10.	电磁阀	diàncífá	n.	solenoid valve

三、视听说　shì-tīng-shuō　Viewing, Listening and Speaking

观看介绍线束编号的相关视频，听师傅讲解不同线束代码的含义，并将不同线束代码与其对应的含义连线，尝试说出电路图中更多代码的含义。**Watch the related video introducing wiring harness codes, listen to the master explaining the meaning of different wiring harness codes, match different wiring harness codes with their corresponding meanings, and try to talk about the meaning of more codes in circuit diagrams.**

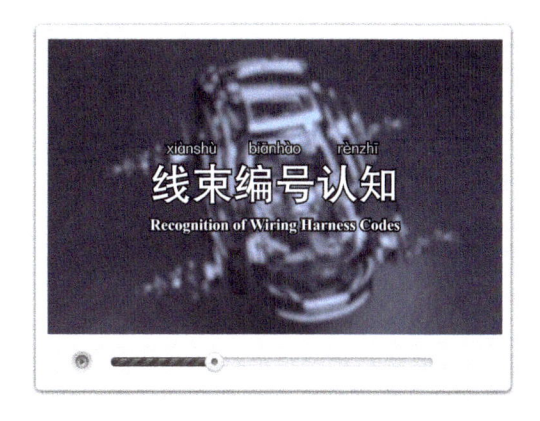

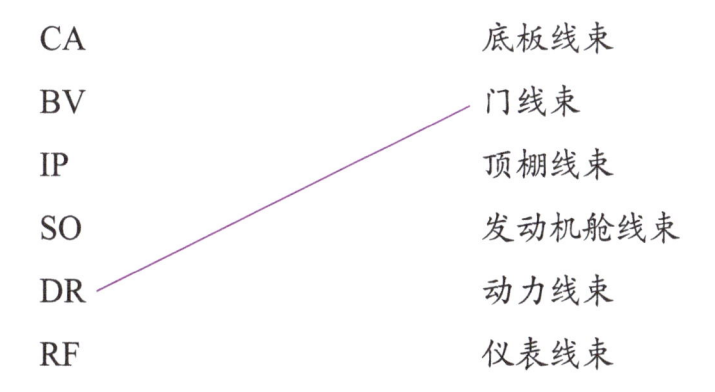

CA	底板线束
BV	门线束
IP	顶棚线束
SO	发动机舱线束
DR	动力线束
RF	仪表线束

四、学以致用　xuéyǐzhìyòng　Practicing What You Have Learnt

观看电路图识读视频，指出保险丝、双绞线和接地的位置。**Watch the video on the intepretation of circuit diagrams, and point out the locations of the fuse, twisted pair, and grounding.**

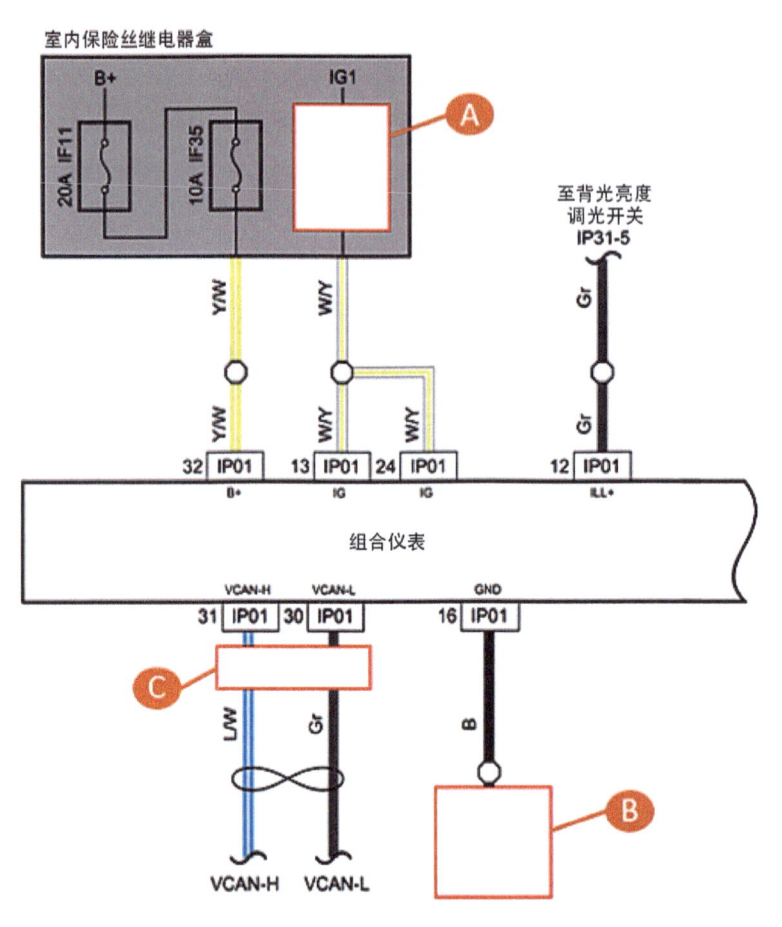

保险丝在＿＿＿＿＿＿，双绞线是＿＿＿＿＿＿，＿＿＿＿＿＿接地。

The fuse is in＿＿＿＿＿, the twisted pair is＿＿＿＿＿, ＿＿＿＿＿ is grounded.

五、小知识 xiǎozhīshi Tips

汽车电路图
Qìchē diànlùtú

汽车电路图可以清晰地表示出汽车各项功能的工作原理和各个电气元件之间的相互联系，汽车电路图上各电气元件和导线旁边都标注有相应的代号。汽车电路图中所有开关及用电器均处于不工作的状态，例如点火开关是断开的、发动机不工作、车灯关闭等。

Circuit Diagram of a Vehicle

The circuit diagram of a vehicle can clearly show the working principle of various functions of a vehicle and the interconnection between various electrical components. The corresponding codes are marked next to various electrical components and leads in the circuit diagram of a vehicle. All switches and electrical appliances in the circuit diagram are in a non-operational state. For example, the ignition switch is disconnected, the engine is not working, and the vehicle lights are off, etc.

补充专业词语 bǔchōng zhuānyè cíyǔ Supplementary Specialized Vocabulary   🎧 06-07

1.	点火开关	diǎnhuǒ kāiguān	phr.	ignition switch
2.	车灯关闭	chēdēng guānbì	phr.	switch off the car lights

第二部分 Part 2
汉字 Chinese Characters

一、汉字知识 Hànzì zhīshi Knowledge about Chinese Characters

1. 汉字的笔画（6） Strokes of Chinese characters (6)

笔画 Strokes	名称 Names	例字 Examples
㇌	横撇弯钩 héngpiěwāngōu	部
㇡	横折折折钩 héngzhézhézhégōu	奶

71

2. 汉字的结构（2） Structures of Chinese characters (2)

结构类型 Structure type	例字 Example	结构图示 Illustration
品字形结构 品-shaped structure	品	⊟

二、汉字认读与书写　Hànzì rèndú yǔ shūxiě　The Recognition and Writing of Chinese Characters

认读下列词语，并试着读写构成词语的汉字。
Recognize the following words, and try to read and write the Chinese characters forming these words.

电路图　　单线制　　动力线束

电			路			图				
单			线			制				
动			力			线			束	

第三部分　Part 3
日常用语 Daily Expressions

① 请原谅。Qǐng yuánliàng. Pardon me, please. / Forgive me, please.
② 不好意思，麻烦你……Bù hǎoyìsi, máfan nǐ… Excuse me, could you please...
③ 我前几天感冒了。Wǒ qián jǐ tiān gǎnmào le. I had a cold several days ago.

第四部分　Part 4
单元实训 Unit Practical Training

电路图识图
Recognition of Circuit Diagrams

实训目的 Training purpose

通过实训，实训人员能够掌握汽车电路图的识图方法，能够根据汽车电路图在车上找到对应电气元件的位置。

Through the practical training, the trainees are able to master the method of recognizing circuit diagrams of vehicles and find the positions of the corresponding electrical components on the vehicle according to the circuit diagram of the vehicle.

实训组织 Training organization

每组 4 人

four trainees in each group

实训步骤 Training steps

❶ 教师展示汽车电路图上的名称代码或者图标符号，引导并启发学员说出代码或符号的含义，并在车上找到对应的位置。

The teacher shows the name codes or icon symbols on the circuit diagram of a vehicle, guides and inspires the trainees to say the meaning of the codes or symbols, and find their corresponding positions on the vehicle.

❷ 将实训人员分成若干小组，每组 4 人。

Divide the trainees into groups of 4.

❸ 实训人员讨论名称代码或者图标符号的含义，寻找其在车上的实际位置，并互相测试。

The trainees discuss the meaning of the name codes or icon symbols, find their actual positions on the vehicle, and test each other.

❹ 小组之间进行比赛，看名称代码或者图标符号说出含义，并确定其在车上的实际位置。

Compete between groups. Look at the name codes or icon symbols to tell the meaning and determine their actual positions on the vehicle.

❺ 教师总结评价，实训结束。

The teacher summarizes and evaluates, and the training ends.

第五部分　Part 5　单元小结 Unit Summary

普通词语　General Vocabulary

1.	整个	zhěnggè	adj.	whole
2.	按照	ànzhào	prep.	according to
3.	清晰	qīngxī	adj.	clear
4.	展示	zhǎnshì	v.	display, demonstrate
5.	款	kuǎn	m.	kind
6.	实际	shíjì	adj.	actual
7.	对应	duìyìng	v.	match
8.	并	bìng	adv.	*used before a negative for emphasis, usually as a retort*
9.	依据	yījù	prep.	according to

词语 Vocabulary

10.	原理	yuánlǐ	n.	principle
11.	合理	hélǐ	adj.	reasonable
12.	布局	bùjú	v.	make overall arrangements, lay out
13.	旁边	pángbiān	n.	side
14.	简写	jiǎnxiě	n.	abbreviation
15.	代表	dàibiǎo	v.	represent
16.	黑色	hēisè	n.	black
17.	这些	zhèxiē	pron.	these
18.	字母	zìmǔ	n.	letter
19.	缩写	suōxiě	n.	abbreviation
20.	表示	biǎoshì	v.	represent, mean
21.	意思	yìsi	n.	meaning
22.	图形	túxíng	n.	graph, figure

专业词语 Specialized Vocabulary

1.	电路图	diànlùtú	n.	circuit diagram
2.	关联	guānlián	v.	be linked
3.	单线制	dānxiànzhì	n.	single-wire system
4.	接地	jiēdì	v.	ground
5.	设备	shèbèi	n.	equipment
6.	并联	bìnglián	v.	make a parallel connection
7.	电气元件	diànqì yuánjiàn	phr.	electrical component
8.	导线	dǎoxiàn	n.	lead
9.	发动机舱线束	fādòngjīcāng xiànshù	phr.	engine compartment wiring harness
10.	动力线束	dònglì xiànshù	phr.	power wiring harness
11.	仪表线束	yíbiǎo xiànshù	phr.	instrument panel wiring harness
12.	底板线束	dǐbǎn xiànshù	phr.	chassis base wiring harness
13.	门线束	mén xiànshù	phr.	door wiring harness
14.	顶棚线束	dǐngpéng xiànshù	phr.	roof wiring harness

cíyǔ 词语 Vocabulary

15.	小负载保险丝	xiǎo fùzài bǎoxiǎnsī	phr.	small load fuse
16.	常闭继电器	chángbì jìdiànqì	phr.	normally closed relay
17.	常开继电器	chángkāi jìdiànqì	phr.	normally open relay
18.	电磁阀	diàncífá	n.	solenoid valve

补充专业词语 Supplementary Specialized Vocabulary

1.	点火开关	diǎnhuǒ kāiguān	phr.	ignition switch
2.	车灯关闭	chēdēng guānbì	phr.	switch off the car lights

jùzi 句子 Sentences

1. 电路图将整个汽车的电路按照关联清晰地展示出来。汽车电路图具有单线制、负极接地、用电设备并联等特点。
2. 汽车电路图上的电气元件依据工作原理，在图中合理布局。
3. 这些图形分别表示接地、小负载保险丝、常闭继电器、温度传感器、蓄电池、常开继电器、电磁阀、加热器。

7

Chōngdiàn xìtǒng
充电系统
Charging Systems

diàndòng qìchē chōngdiàn xìtǒng
电动 汽车 充电 系统
electric vehicle charging systems

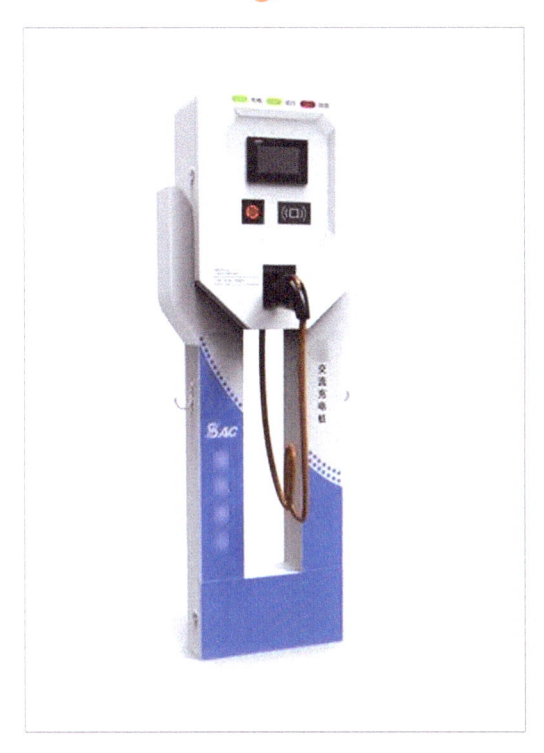

jiāoliú mànsù chōngdiàn xìtǒng
交流（慢速）充电 系统
AC (slow) charging system

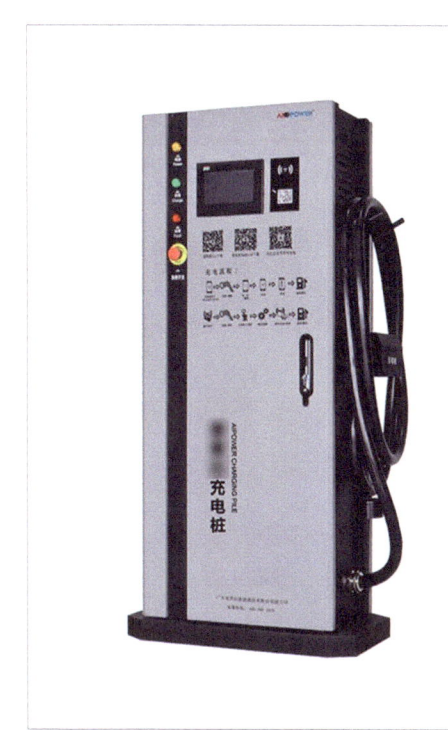

zhíliú kuàisù chōngdiàn xìtǒng
直流（快速）充电 系统
DC (quick) charging system

77

> **题解　Introduction**
>
> 1. 学习内容：电动汽车直流充电和交流充电系统，充电桩接口以及直流充电和交流充电的操作流程。
>   Learning content: The DC charging system and AC charging system of electric vehicles, and the operating process of charging station interface, AC charging and DC charging
> 2. 知识目标：掌握电动汽车充电系统相关核心词汇，了解汉字的笔画"㇆""㇄"和上下结构、上中下结构，学写相关汉字。
>   Knowledge objectives: To master the core vocabulary related to the charging systems of electric vehicles, learn the strokes "㇆", "㇄", the top-bottom structure and the top-middle-bottom structure of Chinese characters, and write the related characters
> 3. 技能目标：掌握电动汽车直流充电和交流充电的操作流程。
>   Skill objective: To master the operating process of AC charging and DC charging of electric vehicles

第一部分　Part 1

课文　Texts

一、热身　rèshēn　Warm-up

1. 给词语选择对应的图片。Choose the corresponding pictures for the words.

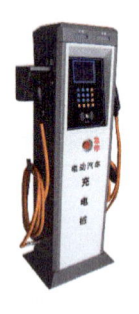

A.

B.

C.

D.

充电系统
Charging Systems 7

E.

F.

chōngdiànzhuāng
❶ 充电桩_____
charging station

chēzài chōngdiànjī
❷ 车载 充电机_____
on-board charger

dònglì xùdiànchí
❸ 动力蓄电池_____
power storage battery

zhuǎnhuànqì
❹ 转换器_____
converter

xiànshù
❺ 线束_____
wiring harness

gāoyā kòngzhìhé
❻ 高压 控制盒_____
high-voltage control box

2. 看视频，了解电动汽车充电系统的类型有哪些，并选择正确的选项。**Watch the video to learn about the types of charging systems of electric vehicles and choose the right options.**

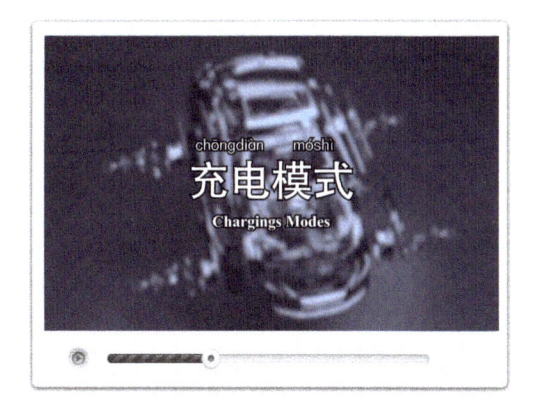

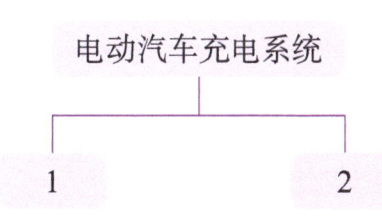

电动汽车充电系统
├─ 1
└─ 2

jiāoliú mànsù chōngdiàn xìtǒng
A. 交流（慢速）充电 系统
AC (slow) charging system

zhōngsù chōngdiàn xìtǒng
B. 中速 充电 系统
medium-speed charging system

zhíliú kuàisù chōngdiàn xìtǒng
C. 直流（快速）充电 系统
DC (quick) charging system

（1）_____   （2）_____

二、课文 kèwén Texts

A 07-01

túdi: 师傅，交流充电系统是不是也叫慢速充电系统？由哪些部件组成？

shīfu: 是的，交流充电系统主要是由交流充电桩或家用交流电源、车载充电机、慢充充电插座、充电枪、高压线束、低压控制线束、高压控制盒、动力蓄电池、整车控制器（VCU）等部件组成。

túdi: 那交流充电很慢，为什么还要这个系统呢？

shīfu: 因为它在成本、安装条件等方面有优势，所以交流充电桩的数量比较多。

译文 yìwén Text in English

Apprentice: Master, is the AC charging system also called a slow charging system? What are the components?

Master: Yes. The AC charging system is mainly composed of AC charging station or household AC power supply, on-board charger, slow charging socket, charging gun, high-voltage wiring harness, low-voltage control wiring harness, high-voltage control box, power storage battery, vehicle control unit (VCU), etc.

Apprentice: Since AC charging is slow, why do we need this system?

Master: Because it has advantages in cost, installation conditions and other aspects, there are more AC charging stations.

普通词语 pǔtōng cíyǔ General Vocabulary 07-02

1.	慢速	mànsù	adj.	low speed
2.	家用	jiāyòng	adj.	for household use, domestic
3.	慢	màn	adj.	slow
4.	为什么	wèi shénme	phr.	why

充电系统
Charging Systems 7

5.	因为	yīnwèi	conj.	because, due to
6.	成本	chéngběn	n.	cost
7.	条件	tiáojiàn	n.	condition
8.	方面	fāngmiàn	n.	aspect
9.	优势	yōushì	n.	advantage
10.	数量	shùliàng	n.	quantity
11.	比较	bǐjiào	adv.	relatively

专业词语 zhuānyè cíyǔ Specialized Vocabulary

07-03

1.	交流充电	jiāoliú chōngdiàn	phr.	AC charging
2.	交流充电桩	jiāoliú chōngdiànzhuāng	phr.	AC charging station
3.	交流电源	jiāoliú diànyuán	phr.	AC power supply
4.	高压线束	gāoyā xiànshù	phr.	high-voltage wiring harness
5.	低压控制线束	dīyā kòngzhì xiànshù	phr.	low-voltage control wiring harness
6.	整车控制器	zhěngchē kòngzhìqì	phr.	vehicle control unit (VCU)

B 07-04

徒弟：师傅，交流充电太慢了。

师傅：你可以试试直流充电，它是快速充电系统。

徒弟：直流充电系统由哪些部件组成？

师傅：直流充电系统主要由直流充电桩、快充插座、高压控制盒、动力蓄电池、整车控制器、高压线束和低压控制线束等组成。

徒弟：直流充电系统是不是对充电桩的安装要求更高？

师傅：是的，你说的没错。

译文 yìwén Text in English

Apprentice: Master, AC charging is too slow.
Master: You can try DC charging. It is a quick charging system.
Apprentice: What are the components of the DC charging system?
Master: It is mainly composed of DC charging station, quick charging socket, high-voltage control box, power storage battery, vehicle control unit, high-voltage wiring harness, low-voltage control wiring harness, etc.
Apprentice: Does the DC charging system have higher requirements for the installation of charging stations?
Master: Yes, you are right.

普通词语 pǔtōng cíyǔ General Vocabulary 🎧 07-05

#				
1.	太	tài	adv.	too
2.	试	shì	v.	try
3.	快速	kuàisù	adj.	fast
4.	要求	yāoqiú	n.	requirement
5.	更	gèng	adv.	more
6.	没错	méi cuò	phr.	correct, right

专业词语 zhuānyè cíyǔ Specialized Vocabulary 🎧 07-06

#				
1.	直流充电	zhíliú chōngdiàn	phr.	DC charging
2.	直流充电桩	zhíliú chōngdiànzhuāng	phr.	DC charging station
3.	快充插座	kuàichōng chāzuò	phr.	quick charging socket

三、视听说 shì-tīng-shuō Viewing, Listening and Speaking

观看介绍充电插头的相关视频，说一说不同国家分别使用哪一种充电插头，并进行连线。**Watch the related video introducing charging sockets, talk about which kind of charging sockets is used in different countries respectively, and match the columns.**

充电插头 chōngdiàn chātóu
Charging Sockets

充电系统 7
Charging Systems

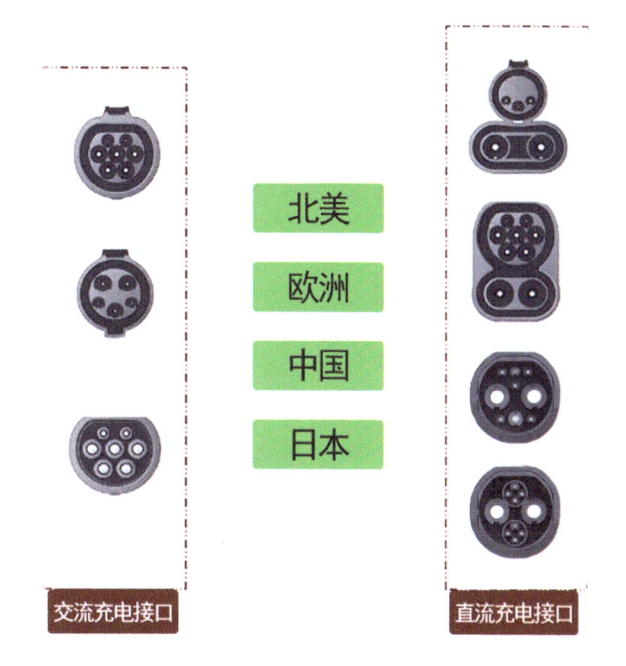

北美
欧洲
中国
日本

交流充电接口　　　直流充电接口

四、学以致用　xuéyǐzhìyòng　Practicing What You Have Learnt

观看介绍充电方式选择的相关视频，判断在以下情境中应该选择直流充电还是交流充电。**Watch the related video introducing the selection of charging modes and judge whether to choose DC charging or AC charging in the following situations.**

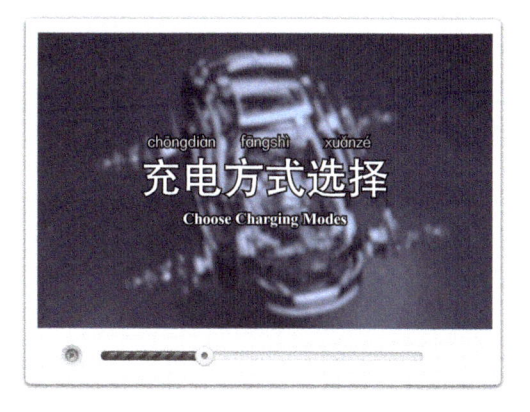

chōngdiàn fāngshì xuǎnzé
充电方式选择
Choose Charging Modes

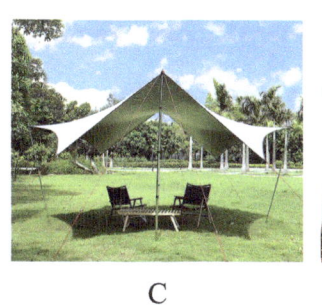

A　　　　　B　　　　　C　　　　　D

zhíliú chōngdiàn:
直流充电：_____

jiāoliú chōngdiàn:
交流充电：_____

DC charging　　　　　　　　　　AC charging

83

五、小知识 xiǎozhīshi Tips

充电 注意 事项
Chōngdiàn zhùyì shìxiàng

1. 频繁 快充 会 缩短 电池 寿命。
   Pínfán kuàichōng huì suōduǎn diànchí shòumìng.

2. 雨天可以给电动 汽车 充电，但在 充电 操作过程 中，要用雨伞 等 物品 进行 遮挡 防护，保证 充电口 和 充电枪 处于干燥 状态。
   Yǔtiān kěyǐ gěi diàndòng qìchē chōngdiàn, dàn zài chōngdiàn cāozuò guòchéng zhōng, yào yòng yǔsǎn děng wùpǐn jìnxíng zhēdǎng fánghù, bǎozhèng chōngdiànkǒu hé chōngdiànqiāng chǔyú gānzào zhuàngtài.

3. 遇雷暴或台风 等 恶劣 天气，尽量不要选择户外 充电，以人身安全 为主。
   Yù léibào huò táifēng děng èliè tiānqì, jǐnliàng búyào xuǎnzé hùwài chōngdiàn, yǐ rénshēn ānquán wéi zhǔ.

4. 尽量 避免 充电器 颠簸 振动，保护好 充电器。
   Jǐnliàng bìmiǎn chōngdiànqì diānbǒ zhèndòng, bǎohù hǎo chōngdiànqì.

Notes for Charging

1. Frequent quick charging will reduce battery life.

2. Electric vehicles can be charged on rainy days, but during the charging operating process, umbrellas or other items should be used as protection to ensure that the charging port and charging gun are in a dry state.

3. In the case of thunderstorms, typhoons or other bad weather, try not to choose outdoor charging, and take personal safety as the main concern.

4. Try to prevent the charger from jolting and vibrating to protect it.

第二部分　Part 2
汉字　Chinese Characters

一、汉字知识　Hànzì zhīshi　Knowledge about Chinese Characters

1. 汉字的笔画（7）Strokes of Chinese characters (7)

笔画 Strokes	名称 Names	例字 Examples
㇆	竖折折钩 shùzhézhégōu	马
㇈	横斜钩 héngxiégōu	风

2. 汉字的结构（3）Structures of Chinese characters (3)

结构类型 Structure types	例字 Examples	结构图示 Illustrations
上下结构 Top-bottom structure	爸 学	▭ ▭
上中下结构 Top-middle-bottom structure	意	☰

二、汉字认读与书写　Hànzì rèndú yǔ shūxiě　The Recognition and Writing of Chinese Characters

认读下列词语，并试着读写构成词语的汉字。
Recognize the following words, and try to read and write the Chinese characters forming these words.

端子　充电器　控制盒　线束

端				子					
充				电				器	
控				制				盒	
线				束					

第三部分　Part 3
日常用语　Daily Expressions

❶ 麻烦你，替我请个假。Máfan nǐ, tì wǒ qǐng gè jià. Could I bother you to ask for leave for me please?

❷ 我被骗了。Wǒ bèi piàn le. I was cheated.

❸ 别着急。Bié zháojí. Don't worry. / Take it easy.

第四部分　Part 4　单元实训 Unit Practical Training

电动汽车充电
Charging of Electric Vehicles

实训目的 Training purpose

通过实训，实训人员能够了解电动汽车直流充电和交流充电的流程和步骤。

Through the practical training, the trainees are able to learn about the procedures and steps of DC charging and AC charging of electric vehicles.

实训组织 Training organization

每组 4 人

four trainees in each group

实训步骤 Training steps

直流充电

DC charging

❶ 关闭车辆的启动开关。

Turn off the start switch of the vehicle.

❷ 打开车辆的直流充电插座，取下防尘罩盖。

Open the DC charging socket of the vehicle and take off the dust cover.

❸ 取下直流充电桩的充电枪，插入车辆上的直流充电插座。

Remove the charging gun from the DC charging station and insert it into the DC charging socket of the vehicle.

❹ 启动直流充电桩，对车辆进行充电（各充电桩的启动步骤不同，通常贴在充电桩上）。

Start the DC charging station to charge the vehicle (different charging stations have different starting steps and instructions are usually attached to the charging stations).

❺ 确认车辆仪表显示正在充电。

Confirm that the vehicle instrument panel indicates it is being charged.

❻ 停止充电。

Stop charging.

❼ 关闭直流充电桩，拔出充电枪（有的车型需要解锁），挂回充电桩上。

Stop the DC charging station, pull out the charging gun (which needs to be unlocked for some vehicle models), and replace it on the charging station.

❽ 盖上防尘罩盖，关上充电插座。

Cover the dust cover and close the charging socket.

交流充电步骤与直流相同，不同是使用交流充电桩时，将充电枪插入车辆的交流充电插座，对车辆进行充电。

The steps of AC charging is the same as that of DC charging, except that when using the AC charging station, the charging gun is inserted into the AC charging socket of the vehicle to charge the vehicle.

❾ 学员互评。

The trainees carry out peer assessment.

❿ 教师总结评价，实训结束。

The teacher summarizes and evaluates, and the training ends.

第五部分　Part 5

单元小结　Unit Summary

词语 cíyǔ Vocabulary

普通词语　General Vocabulary

1.	慢速	mànsù	adj.	low speed
2.	家用	jiāyòng	adj.	for household use, domestic
3.	慢	màn	adj.	slow
4.	为什么	wèi shénme	phr.	why
5.	因为	yīnwèi	conj.	because, due to
6.	成本	chéngběn	n.	cost
7.	条件	tiáojiàn	n.	condition
8.	方面	fāngmiàn	n.	aspect
9.	优势	yōushì	n.	advantage
10.	数量	shùliàng	n.	quantity
11.	比较	bǐjiào	adv.	relatively
12.	太	tài	adv.	too
13.	试	shì	v.	try
14.	快速	kuàisù	adj.	fast
15.	要求	yāoqiú	n.	requirement
16.	更	gèng	adv.	more
17.	没错	méi cuò	phr.	correct, right

专业词语　Specialized Vocabulary

<table>
<tr><td rowspan="9">cíyǔ
词语
Vocabulary</td><td>1.</td><td>交流充电</td><td>jiāoliú chōngdiàn</td><td>phr.</td><td>AC charging</td></tr>
<tr><td>2.</td><td>交流充电桩</td><td>jiāoliú chōngdiàn zhuāng</td><td>phr.</td><td>AC charging station</td></tr>
<tr><td>3.</td><td>交流电源</td><td>jiāoliú diànyuán</td><td>phr.</td><td>AC power supply</td></tr>
<tr><td>4.</td><td>高压线束</td><td>gāoyā xiànshù</td><td>phr.</td><td>high-voltage wiring harness</td></tr>
<tr><td>5.</td><td>低压控制线束</td><td>dīyā kòngzhì xiànshù</td><td>phr.</td><td>low-voltage control wiring harness</td></tr>
<tr><td>6.</td><td>整车控制器</td><td>zhěngchē kòngzhìqì</td><td>phr.</td><td>vehicle control unit (VCU)</td></tr>
<tr><td>7.</td><td>直流充电</td><td>zhíliú chōngdiàn</td><td>phr.</td><td>DC charging</td></tr>
<tr><td>8.</td><td>直流充电桩</td><td>zhíliú chōngdiàn zhuāng</td><td>phr.</td><td>DC charging station</td></tr>
<tr><td>9.</td><td>快充插座</td><td>kuàichōng chāzuò</td><td>phr.</td><td>quick charging socket</td></tr>
</table>

jùzi 句子 Sentences

1. 电动汽车充电系统包括交流（慢速）充电系统和直流（快速）充电系统。
2. 交流充电系统主要是由交流充电桩或家用交流电源、车载充电机、慢充充电插座、充电枪、高压线束、低压控制线束、高压控制盒、动力蓄电池、整车控制器（VCU）等部件组成。
3. 直流充电系统主要由直流充电桩、快充插座、高压控制盒、动力蓄电池、整车控制器、高压线束和低压控制线束等组成。

8 动力蓄电池拆装
Dònglì xùdiànchí chāi zhuāng
Disassembly and Assembly of Power Storage Batteries

juéyuán fánghù zhǔnbèi
绝缘 防护 准备
preparations for insulation protection

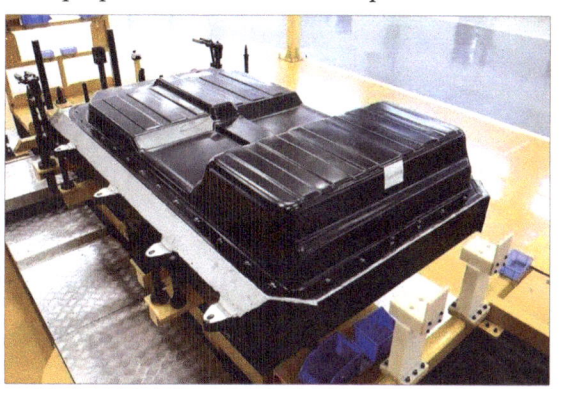

dònglì xùdiànchí chāixiè
动力蓄电池拆卸
disassemly of power storage batteries

dònglì xùdiànchí chāixiè
动力蓄电池拆卸
disassembly of power storage batteries

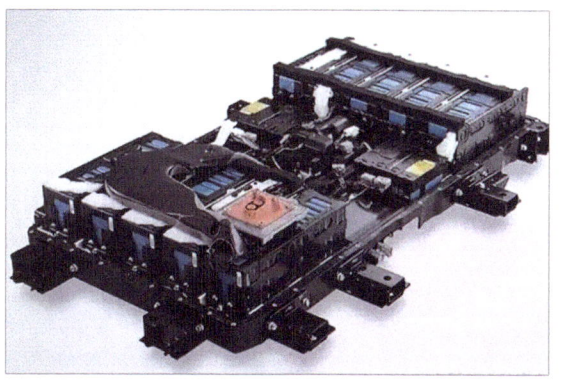

dònglì xùdiànchí zhuāngbèi
动力蓄电池装备
assembly of power storage batteries

题解　Introduction

1. 学习内容：新能源电动汽车动力蓄电池的定义、拆装前提和步骤。
   Learning content: The definition, prerequisites and steps for the disassembly and assembly of power storage batteries of electric vehicles
2. 知识目标：掌握动力蓄电池拆装相关核心词汇，了解汉字的笔画"㇏""㇂"和左右结构、左中右结构，学写相关汉字。
   Knowledge objectives: To master the core vocabulary related to the disassembly and assembly of power storage batteries, learn the strokes "㇏", "㇂", the left-right structure and the left-middle-right structure of Chinese characters, and write the related characters
3. 技能目标：了解蓄电池的定义，熟练掌握动力蓄电池拆装所包含的绝缘、拆卸、装配、SOC 检测四个环节。
   Skill objective: To learn about the definition of storage batteries, master the four steps, namely insulation, disassembly, assembly and SOC test, of the disassembly and assembly of power storage batteries

第一部分　Part 1

课文　Texts

一、热身　rèshēn　Warm-up

1. 给词语选择对应的图片。Choose the corresponding pictures for the words.

1. _____

2. _____

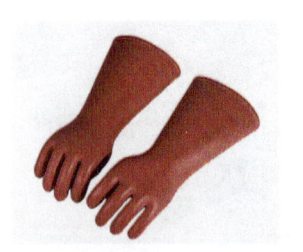

3. _____

4. _____

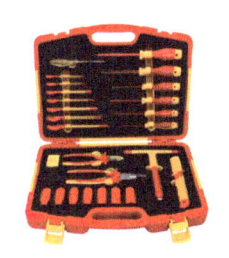

动力蓄电池拆装 8
Disassembly and Assembly of Power Storage Batteries

5.  _____   6. _____

  juéyuán gōngjù   juéyuándiàn   hùmùjìng
A. 绝缘 工具   B. 绝缘垫   C. 护目镜
 insulation tool   insulating mat   goggles

  juéyuán shǒutào   juéyuán fánghùfú   juéyuánxié
D. 绝缘 手套   E. 绝缘防护服   F. 绝缘鞋
 insulating gloves   insulating protective clothing   insulating shoes

2. 观看介绍绝缘防护的相关视频，了解电动汽车动力蓄电池拆装前绝缘防护的准备流程，并排序。
Watch the related video introducing the insulation protection, learn about the preparation process of insulation protection before the disassembly and assembly of power storage batteries of electric vehicles, and put them in order.

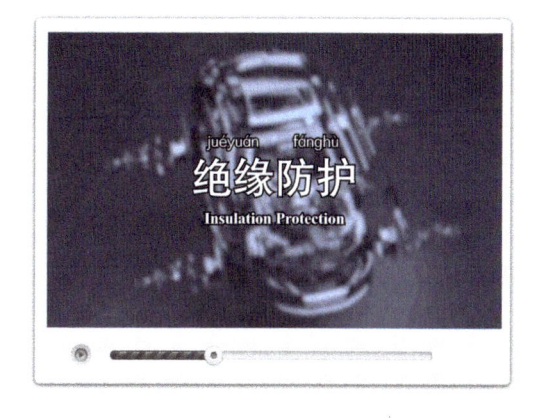

绝缘 fánghù
绝缘防护
Insulation Protection

安全防护措施准备

  wéixiū yíbiǎo   juéyuán gōngjù
A. 维修仪表   B. 绝缘 工具
 repair instrument   insulation tool

91

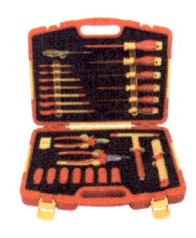

C. 绝缘垫 juéyuándiàn
insulating mat

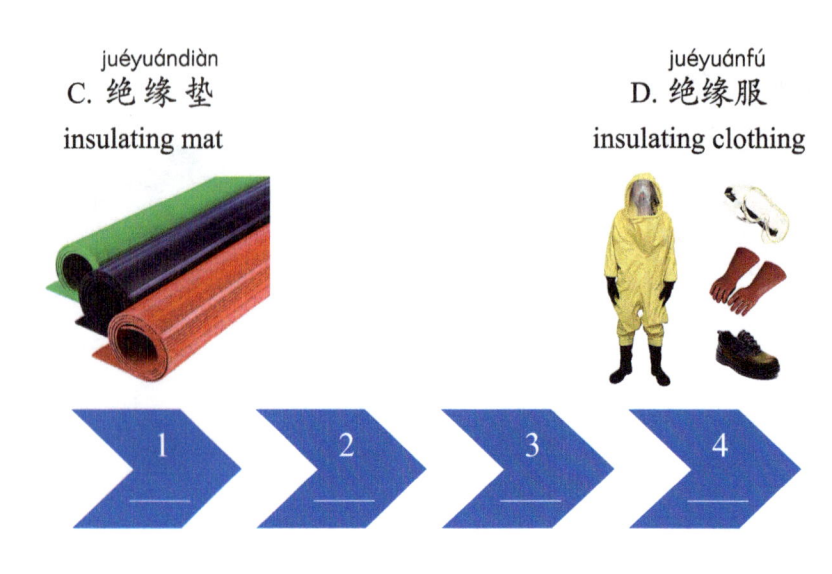

D. 绝缘服 juéyuánfú
insulating clothing

1 → 2 → 3 → 4

二、课文 kèwén Texts

A 09-01

徒弟 túdi：师傅，新能源汽车的动力来源主要有哪些？
Shīfu, xīnnéngyuán qìchē de dònglì láiyuán zhǔyào yǒu nǎxiē?

师傅 shīfu：新能源汽车的动力来源以动力蓄电池为主。实际上，动力蓄电池为电动汽车的动力来源提供的是一种电能。
Xīnnéngyuán qìchē de dònglì láiyuán yǐ dònglì xùdiànchí wéi zhǔ. Shíjì shang, dònglì xùdiànchí wèi diàndòng qìchē de dònglì láiyuán tígōng de shì yì zhǒng diànnéng.

徒弟 túdi：动力蓄电池的工作原理是什么呢？
Dònglì xùdiànchí de gōngzuò yuánlǐ shì shénme ne?

师傅 shīfu：把化学能转化为电能。
Bǎ huàxuénéng zhuǎnhuà wéi diànnéng.

译文 yìwén Text in English

Apprentice: Master, what are the main power sources of new energy vehicles?
Master: The power source of new energy vehicles is mainly power storage batteries. In fact, what the power storage batteries provide for the power source of electric vehicles is a kind of electric energy.
Apprentice: What is the working principle of power storage batteries?
Master: Converting chemical energy into electric energy.

普通词语 pǔtōng cíyǔ General Vocabulary 08-02

1.	实际上	shíjì shang	phr.	in fact, actually
2.	提供	tígōng	v.	provide
3.	种	zhǒng	m.	type, kind

8 动力蓄电池拆装
Disassembly and Assembly of Power Storage Batteries

专业词语 zhuānyè cíyǔ Specialized Vocabulary 08-03

1.	新能源	xīnnéngyuán	n.	new energy
2.	工作原理	gōngzuò yuánlǐ	phr.	working principle
3.	化学能	huàxuénéng	n.	chemical energy

B 09-04

徒弟 (túdi): 在正常情况下，需要对汽车的动力蓄电池进行拆装吗？

师傅 (shīfu): 不需要，只有当动力蓄电池发生故障时才需要进行拆装操作。

徒弟 (túdi): 会有哪些故障表现呢？

师傅 (shīfu): 比如会出现外观扭曲、漏液甚至有焦煳味，或是在充满电的情况下仪表盘仍然显示电量不足等。

译文 yìwén Text in English

Apprentice: Do we need to disassemble and assemble the power storage battery of a vehicle under normal circumstances?

Master: No, we don't. Only when the power storage battery fails does it need to be disassembled and assembled.

Apprentice: What are the possible symptoms of malfunctions?

Master: For example, there will be distorted appearance, liquid leakage and even burnt smell, or the instrument panel still indicates low battery when it is fully charged.

普通词语 pǔtōng cíyǔ General Vocabulary 08-05

1.	情况	qíngkuàng	n.	circumstance
2.	只有	zhǐyǒu	conj.	only
3.	发生	fāshēng	v.	happen
4.	才	cái	adv.	*used to indicate that sth. happens only on certain conditions*

93

5.	会	huì	aux.	be likely to
6.	表现	biǎoxiàn	n.	performance, behaviour
7.	出现	chūxiàn	v.	occur
8.	甚至	shènzhì	conj.	even
9.	焦糊味	jiāohúwèi	n.	burnt smell
10.	仍然	réngrán	adv.	still

专业词语 zhuānyè cíyǔ Specialized Vocabulary 🎧 08-06

1.	拆装	chāi zhuāng	phr.	disassemble and assemble
2.	故障	gùzhàng	n.	breakdown, malfunction
3.	操作	cāozuò	v.	operate
4.	外观	wàiguān	n.	appearance
5.	扭曲	niǔqū	v.	distort
6.	漏液	lòu yè	phr.	liquid leakage
7.	充满电	chōngmǎn diàn	phr.	fully charged
8.	显示	xiǎnshì	v.	show, display
9.	电量不足	diànliàng bùzú	phr.	low battery

三、视听说 shì-tīng-shuō Viewing, Listening and Speaking

1. 观看介绍动力蓄电池拆卸的相关视频，了解动力蓄电池的具体拆卸步骤，并说出每一步的具体操作要求。Watch the related video introducing the disassembly of power storage batteries, understand the specific disassembly steps of power storage batteries, and tell the specific operational requirements for each step.

动力蓄电池拆卸
dònglì xùdiànchí chāixiè
Disassembly of Power Storage Batteries

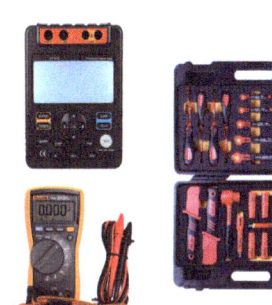

动力蓄电池拆装 **8**

Disassembly and Assembly of Power Storage Batteries

    zhǔnbèi wéixiū gōngjù jí jiǎncè yíbiǎo
① 准备 维修 工具及检测 仪表
prepare repair tools and testing instruments

    chuāndài gāoyā fánghù zhuāngbèi zài dìshang
② 穿戴 高压 防护 装备，在地上
    pūshàng juéyuándiàn
    铺上 绝缘垫
wear high-voltage protective equipment and lay an insulating mat on the ground

③ _____

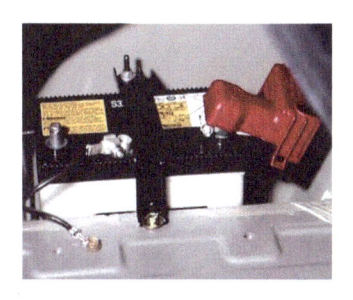

    duànkāi dīyā xùdiànchí de fùjí
④ 断开低压蓄电池的负极
disconnect the negative terminal of the low-voltage storage battery

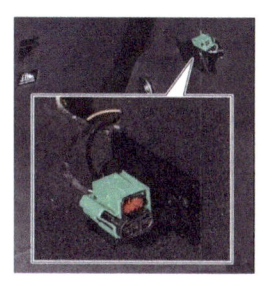

⑤ _____

95

⑥ jǔshēng chēliàng, jiǎnchá dònglì xùdiànchí dǐbù
举升 车辆，检查 动力蓄电池底部
lift up the vehicle and check the bottom of the power storage battery

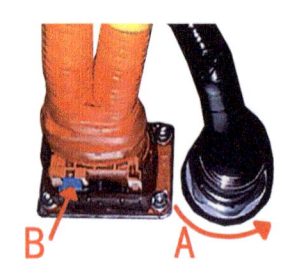

⑦ _____

⑧ chāi dònglì xùdiànchí de gāoyā chājiàn
拆 动力蓄电池的高压插件
remove the high-voltage plug-in of the power storage battery

⑨ jiāng dònglì xùdiànchí jǔshēngchē tuīdào dònglì xù-
将 动力蓄电池举升车 推到动力蓄
diànchí zhèng xiàfāng
电池 正 下方
push the power storage battery lifter right under the power storage battery

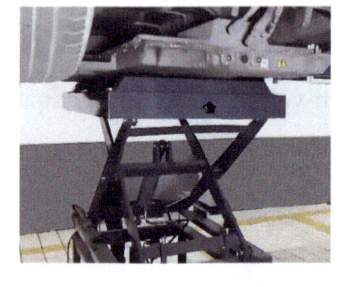

⑩ jǔshēng diànchí jǔshēngchē, yǔ diànchí
举升 电池举升车，与电池
dǐbù jiēchù
底部 接触
lift up the battery lifter to contact with the bottom of the battery

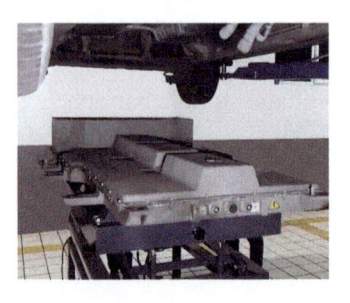

⑪ _____

⑫ _____

96

A. _{chāichú wéixiū kāiguān}
拆除 维修 开关（MSD）
remove the manual service disconnect (MSD)

B. _{guānbì diǎnhuǒ kāiguān}
关闭 点火 开关
turn off the ignition switch

C. _{huǎnmàn xiàjiàng dònglì xùdiànchí jǔshēngchē, jiàngdào xūyào de gāodù hòu, tuīchū dònglì xùdiànchí jǔshēngchē}
缓慢 下降动力蓄电池举升车，降到 需要的高度后， 推出动力蓄电池举升车
slowly lower the power storage battery lifter to the required height, and then push out the power storage battery lifter

D. _{chāixià dònglì xùdiànchí dǐbù}
拆下动力蓄电池底部
remove the bottom of the power storage battery

E. _{chāixià gùdìng luóshuān}
拆下 固定 螺栓
remove the fixed bolts

2. 请试着说出拆卸动力蓄电池的具体步骤。**Please try to tell the specific steps to disassemble power storage batteries.**

四、学以致用　xuéyǐzhìyòng　**Practicing What You Have Learnt**

观看介绍动力蓄电池装配的相关视频，了解动力蓄电池的具体装配步骤，并说出每一步的具体操作要求。**Watch the related video introducing the assembly of power storage batteries, understand the specific assembly steps of power storage batteries, and tell the specific operational requirements for each step.**

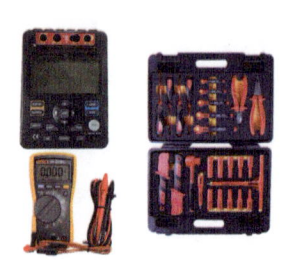

中文＋汽车服务工程技术（中级）

zhǔnbèi wéixiū gōngjù jí jiǎncè yíbiǎo
❶ 准备 维修 工具 及 检测 仪表
prepare repair tools and testing instruments

❷ _____

huǎnmàn shàngshēng dònglì xùdiànchí
❸ 缓慢 上升 动力 蓄电池
jǔshēngchē, tuīrù dònglì diànchí
举升车，推入动力 电池
slowly raise the power storage battery lifter and push in the power battery

❹ _____

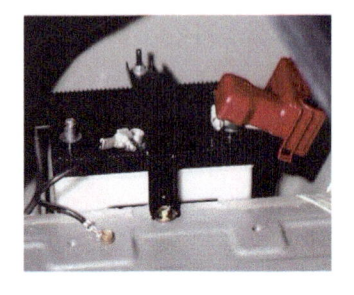

jiēshàng dīyā xùdiànchí de fùjí duānzǐ
❺ 接上 低压 蓄电池的 负极 端子
connect the negative terminal of the low-voltage storage battery

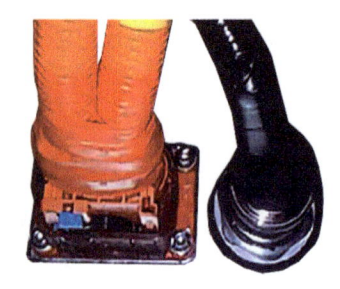

❻ _____

❼ _____

❽ _____

98

A. SOC 检测
   SOC test

B. 确保动力蓄电池箱体的定位销对准底盘上的定位孔，插上定位拴
   ensure that the locating pin of the power storage battery box is aligned with the locating hole on the chassis, and insert the locating bolt

C. 装上动力蓄电池底板
   install the base plate of the power storage battery

D. 穿戴高压防护装备
   wear high-voltage protective equipment

E. 接通动力蓄电池高压插件
   connect the high-voltage plug-in of the power storage battery

五、小知识 xiǎozhīshi Tips

刀片电池

刀片电池是由长96厘米、宽9厘米、高1.35厘米的单体电池，通过阵列的方式排布在一起组成的，由于单体电池像刀片一样插入到电池包，所以被称为刀片电池。

Blade Battery

The blade battery is composed of 96 cm long, 9 cm wide and 1.35 cm high single-cell batteries, which are configured together in an array. Because the single-cell battery is inserted into the battery pack like a blade, it is called a blade battery.

补充专业词语 bǔchōng zhuānyè cíyǔ Supplementary Specialized Vocabulary				08-07
1.	绝缘	juéyuán	v.	insulate
2.	SOC 检测	SOC jiǎncè	phr.	SOC test

第二部分　Part 2
汉字　Chinese Characters

一、汉字知识　Hànzì zhīshi　Knowledge about Chinese Characters

1. 汉字的笔画（8） Strokes of Chinese characters (8)

笔画 Strokes	名称 Names	例字 Examples
ㄴ	竖弯 shùwān	四
ㄱ	横折弯 héngzhéwān	没

2. 汉字的结构（4） Structures of Chinese characters (4)

结构类型 Structure types	例字 Examples	结构图示 Illustrations
左右结构 Left-right structure	银 饭	⊟
左中右结构 Left-middle-right structure	班 微	⊟

二、汉字认读与书写　Hànzì rèndú yǔ shūxiě　The Recognition and Writing of Chinese Characters

认读下列词语，并试着读写构成词语的汉字。
Recognize the following words, and try to read and write the Chinese characters forming these words.

动力　电池　拆卸　装配

| 动 | | | 力 | | | 电 | | | 池 | | |
| 拆 | | | 卸 | | | 装 | | | 配 | | |

第三部分　Part 3　日常用语 Daily Expressions

1. 你不能这样。Nǐ bù néng zhèyàng. You can't be like that.
2. 我马上就到。Wǒ mǎshàng jiù dào. I will be there right away.
3. 让我想想。Ràng wǒ xiǎngxiang. Let me think.

第四部分　Part 4　单元实训 Unit Practical Training

拆装电动汽车动力蓄电池
Disassembly and Assembly of Power Storage Batteries of Electric Vehicles

实训目的 Training purpose

通过实训，实训人员能够熟练掌握并操作拆装电动汽车动力蓄电池。

Through the practical training, the trainees are able to master and operate the disassembly and assembly of power storage batteries of electric vehicles.

实训准备 Training purpose

绝缘维修工具一套、兆欧表/数字式万用表一只、绝缘鞋一双、绝缘手套一副、绝缘服一套、绝缘垫、举升机、动力蓄电池举升车一台、电动汽车一辆。

A set of insulating repair tools, a megger / digital multimeter, a pair of insulating shoes, a pair of insulating gloves, a set of insulating clothing, an insulating mat, a lifter, a power storage battery lifter, and an electric vehicle.

实训方式 Training methods

1. 学员依次按照步骤拆装电动汽车动力蓄电池。

   The trainees take turns to disassemble and assemble the power storage battery of the electric vehicle following the steps.

2. 教师观察学员整个拆装过程，及时发现问题，并予以纠正。

   The teacher observes the whole disassembly and assembly process of the trainees, identify the problems and correct them promptly.

实训步骤 Training steps

拆卸电动汽车动力蓄电池

the disassembly of the power storage battery of an electric vehicle

1. 确认实训准备已经完成。

   Confirm that the training preparations have been completed.

2. 穿戴上绝缘防护服、绝缘鞋、绝缘手套、安全帽、护目镜。在地上铺上绝缘垫。

   Wear insulating protective clothing, insulating shoes, insulating gloves, a safety helmet and goggles.

Lay an insulating mat on the ground.

❸ 关闭开关，断开低压蓄电池的负极，拆除维修开关。
Turn off the switch, disconnect the negative terminal of the low-voltage storage battery, and remove the service switch.

❹ 使用举升机，升起车辆，检查并拆下动力蓄电池底板。
Use the lifter to lift up the vehicle, check and remove the base plate of the power storage battery.

❺ 拆动力蓄电池的高压插件。
Remove the high-voltage plug-in of the power storage battery.

❻ 升高动力蓄电池举升车与电池底部接触。
Lift up the power storage battery lifter to contact with the bottom of the battery.

❼ 拆下动力蓄电池，降下动力蓄电池举升车。
Remove the power storage battery and lower the power storage battery lifter.

装配动力蓄电池步骤与拆卸步骤相反，在举升动力蓄电池时，要确保电池箱体的定位销对准底盘上的定位孔！
The steps of assembling the power storage battery are in reverse order of disassembling. When lifting up the power storage battery, make sure that the locating pin of the battery box is aligned with the locating hole on the chassis!

❽ 教师总结评价，实训结束。
The teacher summarizes and evaluates, and the training ends.

第五部分　Part 5　单元小结　Unit Summary

cíyǔ 词语　Vocabulary

普通词语　General Vocabulary

1.	实际上	shíjì shang	phr.	in fact, actually
2.	提供	tígōng	v.	provide
3.	种	zhǒng	m.	type, kind
4.	情况	qíngkuàng	n.	circumstance
5.	只有	zhǐyǒu	conj.	only
6.	发生	fāshēng	v.	happen
7.	才	cái	adv.	used to indicate that sth. happens only on certain conditions
8.	会	huì	aux.	be likely to
9.	表现	biǎoxiàn	n.	performance, behaviour
10.	出现	chūxiàn	v.	occur
11.	甚至	shènzhì	conj.	even

动力蓄电池拆装
Disassembly and Assembly of Power Storage Batteries

词语 cíyǔ Vocabulary

| 12. | 焦糊味 | jiāohúwèi | n. | burnt smell |
| 13. | 仍然 | réngrán | adv. | still |

专业词语 Specialized Vocabulary

1.	新能源	xīnnéngyuán	n.	new energy
2.	工作原理	gōngzuò yuánlǐ	phr.	working principle
3.	化学能	huàxuénéng	n.	chemical energy
4.	拆装	chāi zhuāng	phr.	disassemble and assemble
5.	故障	gùzhàng	n.	breakdown, malfunction
6.	操作	cāozuò	v.	operate
7.	外观	wàiguān	n.	appearance
8.	扭曲	niǔqū	v.	distort
9.	漏液	lòu yè	phr.	liquid leakage
10.	充满电	chōngmǎn diàn	phr.	fully charged
11.	显示	xiǎnshì	v.	show, display
12.	电量不足	diànliàng bùzú	phr.	low battery

补充专业词语 Supplementary Specialized Vocabulary

| 1. | 绝缘 | juéyuán | v. | insulate |
| 2. | SOC 检测 | SOC jiǎncè | phr. | SOC test |

句子 jùzi Sentences

1. 新能源汽车的动力来源以动力蓄电池为主。
2. 动力蓄电池为电动汽车的动力来源提供的是一种电能。它的工作原理是把化学能转化为电能。
3. 在正常情况下，不需要对汽车的动力蓄电池进行拆装，只有当动力蓄电池发生故障时才需要进行拆装操作。

9

Diàndòng qìchē shìyàn
电动汽车试验
Electric Vehicle Tests

diàndòng qìchē shìyàn xiàngmù
电动 汽车 试验 项目
electric vehicle test items

- zuì gāo chēsù shìyàn
  最 高 车速 试验
  maximum speed test

- jiāsù xìngnéng shìyàn
  加速 性能 试验
  acceleration performance test

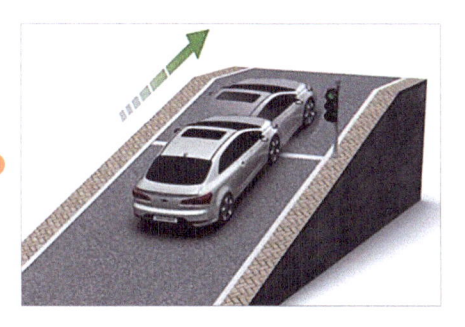

- pá pō shìyàn
  爬坡 试验
  climbing test

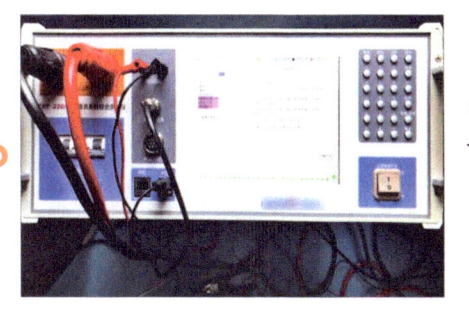

- xùdiànchí wánquán fàngdiàn shìyàn
  蓄电池 完全 放电 试验
  full discharge test of storage batteries

105

题解　Introduction

1. 学习内容：电动汽车的相关试验，包括最高车速试验、30分钟最高车速试验、加速性能试验等。
   Learning content: The relevant tests of electric vehicles, including the maximum speed test, maximum 30 minutes speed test, acceleration performance test and so on

2. 知识目标：掌握电动汽车试验相关核心词汇，了解汉字的笔画"㇉""𠄌"和全包围结构、半包围结构，学写相关汉字。
   Knowledge objectives: To master the core vocabulary related to tests of electric vehicles, learn the strokes "㇉", "𠄌", the fully-enclosed structure and the semi-enclosed structure of Chinese characters, and write the related characters

3. 技能目标：了解电动汽车的基本试验，能够对电动汽车进行基本试验，掌握具体试验步骤以及计算方法。
   Skill objective: To learn about the basic tests of electric vehicles, be able to conduct basic tests for electric vehicles, and master the specific test steps and calculation methods

第一部分　Part 1

课文　Texts

一、热身　rèshēn　Warm-up

1. 给词语选择对应的图片。Choose the corresponding pictures for the words.

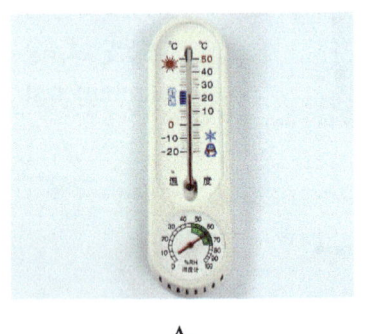

A.

B.

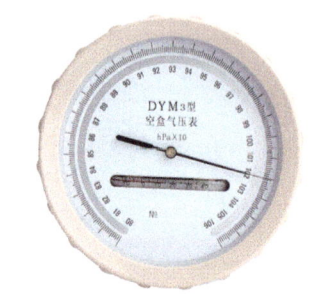

C.

D.

E.

F.

❶ dàqì yālì **大气压力** _____ atmospheric pressure	❷ dàqì wēndù **大气温度** _____ atmospheric temperature
❸ shīdù **湿度** _____ humidity	❹ qìhòu tiáojiàn **气候 条件** _____ climatic conditions
❺ píngjūn fēngsù **平均 风速** _____ average wind speed	❻ lúntāi qìyā **轮胎 气压** _____ tire pressure

2. 观看介绍新能源汽车最高车速试验流程的相关视频，选择正确的操作规范。**Watch the related video introducing the maximum speed test process of new energy vehicles, and choose the correct operation specification.**

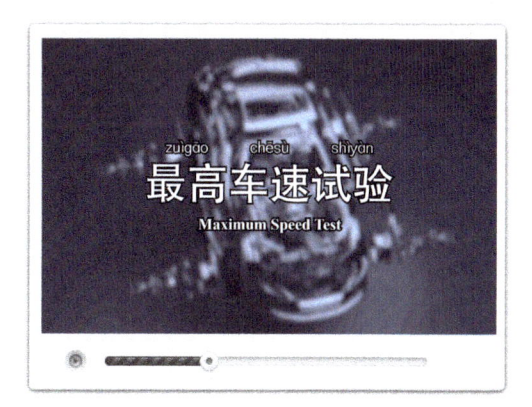

❶ cèshì huánjìng
测试 环境
test environment

A.　　　　　　　　　　　　B.

❷ shìyàn pǎodào
试验 跑道
test track

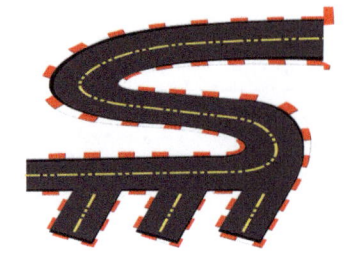

A. 　　　　B.

❸ shìyàn cìshù
试验 次数
number of tests

A. 　　　　B.

❹ chēsù jìsuàn, shìyàn jùlí wéi 1 qiānmǐ
车速 计算，试验距离为 1 千米
speed calculation, the test distance is 1 km

速度 =3600/t_1	速度 =3600/t_2	速度 =3600/t，t=（t_1+t_2）/2
A	B	C

二、课文　kèwén　Texts

A 🎧 09-01

túdi: Shīfu, 30 fēnzhōng zuì gāo chēsù shìyàn yào zhǔnbèi shénme?
徒弟：师傅，30 分钟 最高车速试验 要 准备 什么？

shīfu: Xūyào jiāng chēliàng jiāzài dào shìyàn zhìliàng, bǎozhèng zàihè fēnbù jūnyún.
师傅：需要将 车辆 加载到 试验 质量，保证 载荷分布均匀。

túdi: Zhǔnbèi hǎo le, ránhòu ne?
徒弟：准备 好了，然后呢？

shīfu: Shìyàn chēliàng yǐ 30 fēnzhōng zuì gāo chēsù xíngshǐ 30 fēnzhōng. Ruò chēsù fāshēng
师傅：试验 车辆以 30 分钟 最高车速行驶 30 分钟。若车速发生

		biànhuà, tōngguò cǎi jiāsù tàbǎn lái bǔcháng.
		变化，通过 踩加速踏板来补偿。
túdi:		Hǎo de, shīfu. Zài jìlù xíngshǐ lǐchéng zhīhòu ne?
徒弟：		好的，师傅。在记录行驶里程之后呢？
shīfu:		Yòng gōngshì jìsuàn píngjūn 30 fēnzhōng zuì gāo chēsù.
师傅：		用 公式 计算平均30分钟 最高车速。

译文 yìwén Text in English

Apprentice: Master, what should I prepare for the maximum 30 minutes speed test?

Master: It is necessary to load the vehicle to the test mass and ensure uniform load distribution.

Apprentice: Ready, and then?

Master: The test vehicle should be driven at the maximum 30 minutes speed for 30 minutes. If the speed changes, it should be compensated by stepping on the accelerator pedal.

Apprentice: OK. Master, what shall I do after recording the mileage?

Master: Use the formula to calculate the maximum 30 minutes speed average.

普通词语 pǔtōng cíyǔ General Vocabulary   🎧 09-02

1.	保证	bǎozhèng	v.	ensure, gurantee
2.	分布均匀	fēnbù jūnyún	phr.	uniform distribution
3.	然后	ránhòu	conj.	then
4.	若	ruò	conj.	if
5.	变化	biànhuà	v.	change
6.	通过	tōngguò	prep.	through
7.	踩	cǎi	v.	step on
8.	记录	jìlù	v.	record
9.	之后	zhīhòu	n.	later
10.	公式	gōngshì	n.	formula
11.	平均	píngjūn	v.	average

专业词语 zhuānyè cíyǔ Specialized Vocabulary   🎧 09-03

1.	最高车速	zuì gāo chēsù	phr.	maximum speed
2.	试验	shìyàn	n.	test
3.	加载	jiāzài	v.	load
4.	质量	zhìliàng	n.	quality
5.	载荷	zàihè	n.	load

6.	加速踏板	jiāsù tàbǎn	n.	accelerator pedal
7.	补偿	bǔcháng	v.	compensate
8.	里程	lǐchéng	n.	mileage
9.	计算	jìsuàn	v.	calculate

B 09-04

túdi: 师傅，汽车 0~50km/h 加速性能试验要准备什么？

shīfu: 需要将车辆加载到试验质量，保证载荷分布均匀。

túdi: 准备好了，然后呢？

shīfu: 车辆在测试起始位置启动以后将车辆加速到（50±1）km/h，记录车辆开始加速到达到（50±1）km/h 的时间 t_1，然后做一次反方向的试验，并记录通过的时间 t_2，两个时间的平均值就是加速时间。

túdi: 好的，师傅。那 50~80km/h 的加速试验也是这样做吗？

shīfu: 是的。

译文 yìwén Text in English

Apprentice: Master, what do I need to prepare for the 0-50km/h acceleration performance test?

Master: It is necessary to load the vehicle to the test mass and ensure uniform load distribution.

Apprentice: Ready, and then?

Master: After the vehicle is started at the starting point of the test, accelerate the vehicle to (50 ± 1) km/h, record the time t_1 it takes from starting acceleration to reaching (50±1) km/h, then conduct a test in reverse direction, and record the time t_2. The average value of these two times is the acceleration time.

Apprentice: I see. Master, is the 50-80km/h acceleration test done the same way?

Master: Yes, it is.

电动汽车试验 9
Electric Vehicle Tests

普通词语 pǔtōng cíyǔ General Vocabulary   🎧 09-05

1.	起始位置	qǐshǐ wèizhì	phr.	starting position
2.	以后	yǐhòu	n.	afterwards
3.	达到	dádào	v.	reach
4.	这样	zhèyàng	pron.	such

专业词语 zhuānyè cíyǔ Specialized Vocabulary   🎧 09-06

1.	加速	jiāsù	v.	accelerate
2.	性能	xìngnéng	n.	performance
3.	反方向	fǎn fāngxiàng	phr.	reverse direction
4.	平均值	píngjūn zhí	phr.	average value

三、视听说 shì-tīng-shuō   Viewing, Listening and Speaking

1. 观看介绍电动汽车爬坡试验的相关视频，选择爬坡试验操作流程的名称，并说出注意事项。**Watch the related video introducing the climbing test of electric vehicles, select the names of the operating steps of the climbing test, and talk about the precautions.**

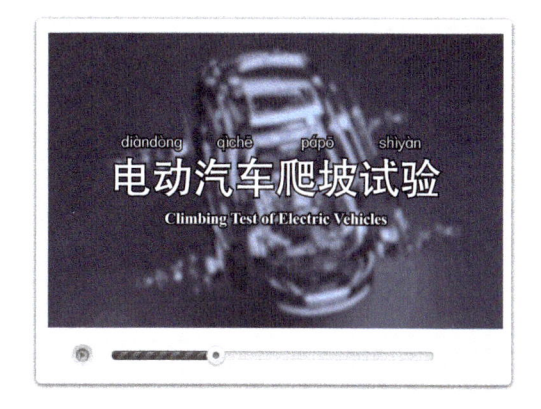

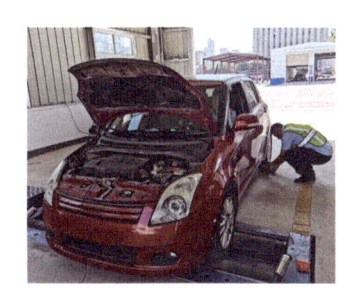

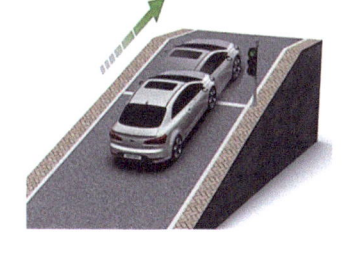

① _____

② _____

111

③ _____

  chíxù xíngshǐ 1km de zuì gāo wěndìng chēsù, jìlù t₁
④ 持续 行驶 1km 的 最 高 稳 定 车速，记录 t₁
  record t₁ for maximum stable speed for continuous driving for 1km

⑤ _____   ⑥ _____

  jiāng chēliàng zhì yú cègōngjī, tiáozhěng dào shìyàn chēliàng de zhìliàng
A. 将 车辆 置 于 测功机，调整 到 试验 车辆 的 质量
  place the vehicle on the dynamometer, and adjust it to the mass of test vehicles

  tiáozhěng cègōngjī, zēngjiā yí gè xiāngdāng yú 12% pōdù de fùjiā zàihè
B. 调整 测功机，增加一个 相当 于 12% 坡度 的 附加 载荷
  adjust the dynamometer to add an additional load equivalent to a 12% slope

  tiáozhěng cègōngjī, zēngjiā yí gè xiāngdāng yú 4% pōdù de fùjiā zàihè
C. 调整 测功机，增加一个 相当 于 4% 坡度 的 附加 载荷
  adjust the dynamometer to add an additional load equivalent to a 4% slope

  chíxù xíngshǐ 1km de zuì gāo wěndìng chēsù, jìlù t₂
D. 持续 行驶 1km 的 最 高 稳 定 车速，记录 t₂
  record t₂ for maximum stable speed for continuous driving for 1km

  jiǎnchá
E. 检查
  check

  jiāng shìyàn chēliàng jiāzài dào shìyàn zhìliàng, bǎozhèng zàihé fēnbù jūnyún
F. 将 试验 车辆 加载 到 试验 质量，保证 载荷 分布 均匀
  load the test vehicle to the test mass and ensure uniform load distribution

2. 请试着说出爬坡试验的具体步骤。**Please try to tell the specific steps of the climbing test.**

四、学以致用　xuéyǐzhìyòng　Practicing What You Have Learnt

观看介绍动力蓄电池完全放电试验的相关视频，排列出正确的操作顺序。**Watch the related video introducing the full discharge test of power storage batteries and arrange the correct sequence of operations.**

　　　　　chēliàng tíngfàng 30 fēnzhōng
A. 车辆 停放 30 分钟
　　park the vehicle for 30 minutes

　　　　　xìnhào zhuāngzhì tíshì tíng chē
B. 信号 装置 提示停车
　　the signal device prompts to stop

　　　yǐ 30 fēnzhōng zuì gāo chēsù de 70% de
C. 以 30 分钟 最高车速的 70%的
　　sùdù　huīfù xíngshǐ
　　速度 恢复行驶
　　resume driving at 70% of the maximum
　　30 minutes speed

　　　　jìsuàn zǒng de xíngshǐ lǐchéng
D. 计算总的行驶里程
　　calculate the total mileage

wánchéng 30 fēnzhōng zuì gāo chēsù shìyàn
E. 完成 30 分钟 最高 车速 试验
complete the maximum 30 minutes speed test

□ → □ → □ → □ → □ → □

五、小知识　xiǎozhīshi　Tips

Xīnnéngyuán qìchē de shìyàn mùdì
新能源 汽车的试验目的

30 fēnzhōng zuì gāo chēsù shìyàn hé zuì gāo chēsù shìyàn dàibiǎo qìchē de jiāsù xìngnéng.
1. 30 分钟 最高车速试验和最高车速试验代表汽车的加速性能。

Jiāsù xìngnéng shìyàn hé pá pō chēsù shìyàn tǐxiànle diàndòngqìchē dònglì xìngnéng.
2. 加速 性能 试验和爬坡车速试验体现了电动汽车动力 性能。

Xùdiànchí wánquán fàngdiàn shìyàn tǐxiànle dònglì xùdiànchí xìngnéng.
3. 蓄电池 完全 放电试验体现了动力蓄电池 性能。

Purpose of New Energy Vehicle Tests

1. The maximum 30 minutes speed test and the maximum speed test represent the acceleration performance of vehicles.

2. The acceleration performance test and the climbing speed test reflect the power performance of electric vehicles.

3. The full discharge test of storage batteries reflects the performance of power storage batteries.

补充专业词语 bǔchōng zhuānyè cíyǔ　Supplementary Specialized Vocabulary　🎧 09-07

1.	湿度	shīdù	n.	humidity
2.	轮胎气压	lúntāi qìyā	phr.	tire pressure
3.	跑道	pǎodào	n.	track
4.	测功机	cègōngjī	n.	dynamometer

电动汽车试验 9
Electric Vehicle Tests

第二部分　Part 2　汉字 Chinese Characters

一、汉字知识　Hànzì zhīshi　Knowledge about Chinese Characters

1. 汉字的笔画（9）Strokes of Chinese characters (9)

笔画 Strokes	名称 Names	例字 Examples
㇇	横折折撇 héngzhézhépiě	延、建
㇋	竖折撇 shùzhépiě	专

2. 汉字的结构（5）Structures of Chinese characters (5)

结构类型 Structure types	例字 Examples	结构图示 Illustrations
全包围结构 Fully-enclosed structure	国	▢
半包围结构 Semi-enclosed structure	医 边 问 唐 凶	▢ ▢ ▢ ▢ ▢

二、汉字认读与书写　Hànzì rèndú yǔ shūxiě　The Recognition and Writing of Chinese Characters

认读下列词语，并试着读写构成词语的汉字。
Recognize the following words, and try to read and write the Chinese characters forming these words.

试验　车速　性能　载荷

| 试 | | | 验 | | | 车 | | | 速 | | |
| 性 | | | 能 | | | 载 | | | 荷 | | |

第三部分　Part 3　日常用语 Daily Expressions

❶ 我该怎么办？Wǒ gāi zěnme bàn? What should I do?

115

❷ 麻烦你，告诉我他的电话号码。Máfan nǐ, gàosu wǒ tā de diànhuà hàomǎ. Excuse me, could you please tell me his phone number?

❸ 真不好意思，我忘了给你打电话。Zhēn bù hǎoyìsi, wǒ wàngle gěi nǐ dǎ diànhuà. Sorry, I forgot to phone you.

第四部分 Part 4　单元实训 Unit Practical Training

电动汽车基本试验
Basic Tests of Electric Vehicles

实训目的 Training purpose

通过实训，实训人员能够了解电动汽车的性能试验，能够对电动汽车进行性能试验。

Through the practical training, the trainees are able to understand performance tests of electric vehicles and carry out performance tests of electric vehicles.

实训准备 Training steps

电动汽车若干辆

several electric vehicles

实训步骤 Training steps

❶ 实训内容：分组完成电动汽车性能试验，包括30分钟最高车速试验、蓄电池完全放电、最高车速、加速性能试验、爬坡车速试验。

Training content: Complete performance tests of electric vehicles in groups, including maximum 30 minutes speed test, full discharge of storage batteries, maximum speed, acceleration performance test and climbing speed test.

❷ 分组讨论，每组3-5人。

Discuss in groups, with 3-5 trainees in each group.

❸ 每组学员合作完成一个试验项目，然后各组轮换，完成全部项目。

Each group of trainees cooperate to complete a test project, and then the groups rotate to complete all the projects.

❹ 教师总结评价，实训结束。

The teacher summarizes and evaluates, and the training ends.

第五部分　Part 5

单元小结　Unit Summary

词语 cíyǔ Vocabulary

普通词语　General Vocabulary

1.	保证	bǎozhèng	v.	ensure, gurantee
2.	分布均匀	fēnbù jūnyún	phr.	uniform distribution
3.	然后	ránhòu	conj.	then
4.	若	ruò	conj.	if
5.	变化	biànhuà	v.	change
6.	通过	tōngguò	prep.	through
7.	踩	cǎi	v.	step on
8.	记录	jìlù	v.	record
9.	之后	zhīhòu	n.	later
10.	公式	gōngshì	n.	formula
11.	平均	píngjūn	v.	average
12.	起始位置	qǐshǐ wèizhì	phr.	starting position
13.	以后	yǐhòu	n.	afterwards
14.	达到	dádào	v.	reach
15.	这样	zhèyàng	pron.	such

专业词语　Specialized Vocabulary

1.	最高车速	zuì gāo chēsù	phr.	maximum speed
2.	试验	shìyàn	n.	test
3.	加载	jiāzài	v.	load
4.	质量	zhìliàng	n.	quality
5.	载荷	zàihè	n.	load
6.	加速踏板	jiāsù tàbǎn	n.	accelerator pedal
7.	补偿	bǔcháng	v.	compensate
8.	里程	lǐchéng	n.	mileage
9.	计算	jìsuàn	v.	calculate
10.	加速	jiāsù	v.	accelerate
11.	性能	xìngnéng	n.	performance
12.	反方向	fǎn fāngxiàng	phr.	reverse direction
13.	平均值	píngjūn zhí	phr.	average value

	补充专业词语		Supplementary Specialized Vocabulary	
cíyǔ **词语** Vocabulary	1. 湿度	shīdù	n.	humidity
	2. 轮胎气压	lúntāi qìyā	phr.	tire pressure
	3. 跑道	pǎodào	n.	track
	4. 测功机	cègōngjī	n.	dynamometer

jùzi
句子
Sentences

1. 30分钟最高车速试验首先需要将车辆加载到试验质量，保证载荷分布均匀。
2. 若30min车速发生变化，必须通过踩加速踏板来补偿。
3. 车辆在测试起始位置启动以后将车辆加速到（50±1）km/h，记录车辆开始加速到达到（50±1）km/h的时间t_1，然后做一次反方向的试验，并记录通过的时间t_2，两个时间的平均值就是加速时间。

10 Diàndòng qìchē xiāoshòu
电动汽车销售
Electric Vehicle Sales

diàndòng qìchē xiāoshòu
电动汽车销售
electric vehicle sales

- chǎnpǐn tuījiàn
  产品 推荐
  product recommendation

- shì chéng shì jià
  试 乘 试 驾
  test drive

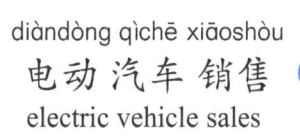

- chōngdiàn fāngfǎ zhǐdǎo
  充电 方法指导
  guidance on charging methods

- yìyì chǔlǐ
  异议处理
  settlement of objections

- qiānyuē yǔ jiāo chē
  签约与交车
  contract signing and delivery of vehicles

119

题解 Introduction

1. 学习内容：电动汽车销售流程和销售技巧。
   Learning content: The process and skills of electric vehicle sales
2. 知识目标：掌握电动汽车销售相关核心词汇，学习汉字的笔画（总表）、笔顺（总表）和结构（总表），学写相关汉字。
   Knowledge objectives: To master the core vocabulary related to electric vehicle sales, learn the general tables of strokes, stroke orders and structures of Chinese characters, and write the related characters
3. 技能目标：能够使用对应电动汽车充电、安全、电池衰减、续航里程、价格等问题的语言技能进行应对，并能分析问题产生的原因。
   Skill objective: To be able to handle charging, safety, battery attenuation, range, price and other problems of electric vehicles with corresponding language skills, and analyze the causes of these problems

第一部分 Part 1

课文 Texts

一、热身 rèshēn Warm-up

1. 给词语选择对应的图片。Choose the corresponding pictures for the words.

A.

B.

C.

D.

　　　chōngdiàn wèntí
❶ 充电 问题＿＿＿＿＿＿＿
    charging problem

　　　zhěngchē ānquán
❷ 整车 安全＿＿＿＿＿＿＿
    vehicle safety

③ 电池 衰减_____
diànchí shuāijiǎn
battery attenuation

④ 续航 里程_____
xùháng lǐchéng
range

2. 观看介绍电动汽车销售流程的相关视频，选择对应流程。**Watch the related video introducing the sales process of electric vehicles, and select the corresponding process.**

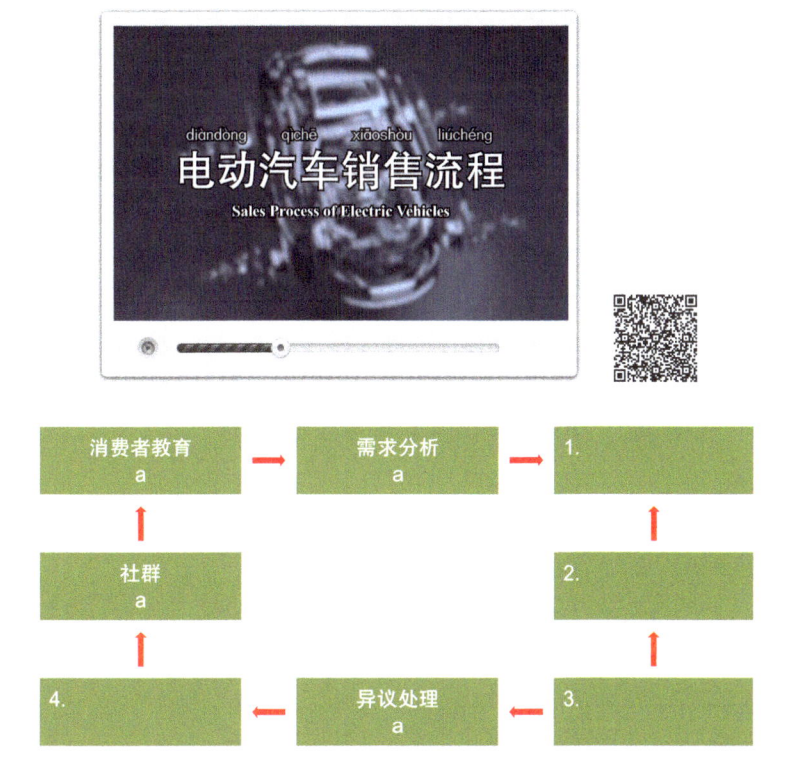

```
消费者教育 a  →  需求分析 a  →  1.
    ↑                              ↓
  社群 a                          2.
    ↑                              ↓
   4.        ←   异议处理 a    ←   3.
```

A. 充电 指导
chōngdiàn zhǐdǎo
charging guidance

B. 签约 交车
qiānyuē jiāo chē
contract signing and delivery of vehicles

C. 试 乘 试 驾
shì chéng shì jià
test drive

D. 产品 推荐
chǎnpǐn tuījiàn
product recommendation

三、课文 kèwén Texts

A 🎧 10-01

销售员 xiāoshòuyuán：欢迎 光临 4S 店，这么 热 的 天，辛苦 您 亲自 过来，先 到 这边 休息 一下，您 是 喝 咖啡 还是 喝 茶 呢？我 是 李伟，您 的 专属 销售 顾问，这 是 我 的 名片。

Huānyíng guānglín 4S diàn, zhème rè de tiān, xīnkǔ nín qīnzì guòlái, xiān dào zhè biān xiūxi yíxià, nín shì hē kāfēi háishi hē chá ne? Wǒ shì Lǐ Wěi, nín de zhuānshǔ xiāoshòu gùwèn, zhè shì wǒ de míngpiàn.

	kèhù:	Xīnnéngyuán qìchē yǔ rányóu qìchē xiāng bǐ yǒu shénme yōushì?		
	客户:	新能源汽车与燃油汽车相比有什么优势?		
	xiāoshòuyuán:	Tā chōngdiàn fāngbiàn, wěndìngxìng qiáng, zhìnénghuà gāo, cāozuò jiǎnyì, mǎi		
	销售员:	它充电方便,稳定性强,智能化高,操作简易,买		
		chē yǒu bǔtiē, bìngqiě shǐyòng hé bǎoyǎng chéngběn dōu jiào dī.		
		车有补贴,并且使用和保养成本都较低。		

译文 yìwén Text in English

Salesperson: Welcome to our 4S store. Thanks for visiting in person on such a hot day. Have a rest over here first. What would you like, coffee or tea? I'm Li Wei, your exclusive sales consultant. Here is my business card.

Customer: What are the advantages of new energy vehicles over fuel vehicles?

Salesperson: It is convenient to charge, highly stable and intelligent. The vehicle is easy to operate and subsidized for buying, with low use and maintenance costs.

普通词语 pǔtōng cíyǔ General Vocabulary 🎧 10-02

1.	欢迎光临	huānyíng guānglín	phr.	welcome
2.	店	diàn	n.	store
3.	这么	zhème	pron.	such
4.	天	tiān	n.	weather
5.	辛苦	xīnkǔ	v.	go through hardships
6.	亲自	qīnzì	adv.	in person
7.	过来	guòlái	v.	come over
8.	先	xiān	adv.	first
9.	这边	zhè biān	phr.	here, this side
10.	休息	xiūxi	v.	have a rest
11.	喝	hē	v.	drink
12.	咖啡	kāfēi	n.	coffee
13.	茶	chá	n.	tea
14.	名片	míngpiàn	n.	business card
15.	相比	xiàng bǐ	phr.	compare with each other
16.	强	qiáng	adj.	superior
17.	简易	jiǎnyì	adj.	easy
18.	较低	jiào dī	phr.	relatively low

电动汽车销售
Electric Vehicle Sales

专业词语 zhuānyè cíyǔ Specialized Vocabulary 🎧 10-03

1.	专属	zhuānshǔ	adj.	exclusive
2.	销售顾问	xiāoshòu gùwèn	phr.	sales consultant
3.	充电方便	chōngdiàn fāngbiàn	phr.	be easy to charge
4.	稳定性	wěndìngxìng	n.	stability
5.	智能化	zhìnénghuà	v.	be intelligent
6.	补贴	bǔtiē	n.	subsidy
7.	保养	bǎoyǎng	v.	maintain, keep in good repair

B 🎧 10-04

客户：新能源汽车安全吗？

销售员：非常安全。车身外壳完全是以汽车标准生产制造的，并且车辆配有ABS、安全气囊、防撞钢梁等一系列安全配置，在安全性能上取得了很好的兼顾。

客户：无论如何，你们优惠幅度太低了，超出预算了。

销售员：价格固然重要，但您更应该先选好你最喜欢的车型和配置，确定了之后咱们再来详细谈谈价格，您看可以吗？

译文 yìwén Text in English

Customer: Are new energy vehicles safe?

Salesperson: Very safe. The body shell is manufactured in complete accordance with automotive standards, and the vehicle is equipped with a series of safety devices, such as ABS, airbag, anti-collision beam, etc. It has taken all factors regarding safety performance into consideration.

Customer: Anyway, your preferential margin is too low, and it is beyond my budget.

Salesperson: Though the price is important, you should choose your favorite model and configuration first, and then we can talk about the price in detail, is that OK?

普通词语 pǔtōng cíyǔ General Vocabulary 🎧 10-05

1.	完全	wánquán	adv.	completely, totally
2.	取得	qǔdé	v.	gain
3.	兼顾	jiāngù	v.	give consideration to two or more things
4.	无论如何	wúlùn rúhé	phr.	anyway
5.	价格	jiàgé	n.	price
6.	固然	gùrán	conj.	no doubt
7.	选	xuǎn	v.	choose
8.	确定	quèdìng	v.	confirm
9.	详细	xiángxì	adj.	detailed
10.	谈	tán	v.	talk

专业词语 zhuānyè cíyǔ Specialized Vocabulary 🎧 10-06

1.	外壳	wàiké	n.	outer casing, shell
2.	汽车标准	qìchē biāozhǔn	phr.	automotive standards
3.	制造	zhìzào	v.	manufacture
4.	配	pèi	v.	equip
5.	安全气囊	ānquán qìnáng	phr.	airbag
6.	防撞钢梁	fáng zhuàng gāngliáng	phr.	anti-collision beam
7.	安全配置	ānquán pèizhì	phr.	safety configuration
8.	安全性能	ānquán xìngnéng	phr.	safety performance
9.	优惠幅度	yōuhuì fúdù	phr.	preferential margin
10.	超出预算	chāochū yùsuàn	phr.	beyond the budget
11.	车型	chēxíng	n.	vehicle model
12.	配置	pèizhì	n.	configuration

电动汽车销售
Electric Vehicle Sales

三、视听说　shì-tīng-shuō　Viewing, Listening and Speaking

1. 观看介绍电动汽车促销方式的相关视频，给图片选出对应的促销方式，并说出促进新能源汽车销售的方式。Watch the related video introducing promotion methods for electric vehicles, choose the corresponding promotion methods for the pictures, and tell the methods to promote sales of new energy vehicles.

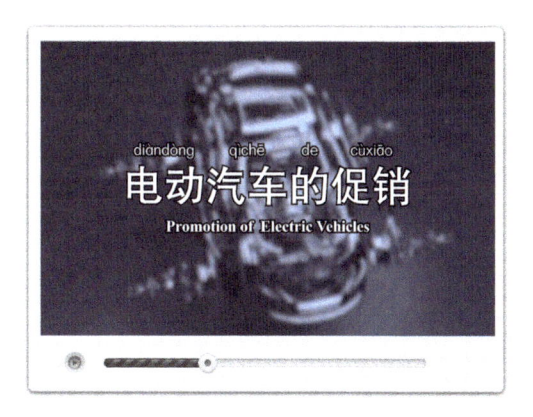

diàndòng qìchē de cùxiāo
电动汽车的促销
Promotion of Electric Vehicles

1.　　　　　　　2.　　　　　　　3.

4.　　　　　　　5.

yōushì gōngnéng bǐduì
A. 优势 功能 比对
comparison of advantages and functions

wánshàn xiāoshòuqúdào
B. 完善 销售 渠道
improving sales channels

guǎnggào xuānchuán
C. 广告 宣传
advertising

chēzhǎn
D. 车展
auto show

cùxiāo huódòng
E. 促销 活动
sales promotion

2. 请试着说出促进新能源汽车销售的三种方式。Please try to tell three methods of promoting sales of new energy vehicles.

四、学以致用　xuéyǐzhìyòng　Practicing What You Have Learnt

看视频，判断下列情况是什么原因造成电动汽车续航里程问题的。Watch the video and judge what causes the range problem of electric vehicles in the following situations.

❶ chíxù shǐyòng cǎinuǎn kōngtiáo 2KW/ xiǎoshí
持续使用　采暖　空调　2KM/ 小时

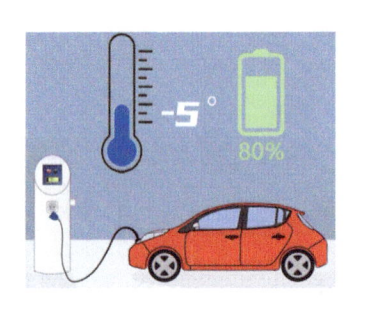

❷ qìwēn -5℃ shí zhǐ néng chōngdiàn 80%
气温 -5℃时只能　充电 80%

车内人员满载

咯咯　哒哒

❸ chē shang zuòmǎnle rén
车　上　坐满了人

A. qìchē zàizhòng
汽车载重
auto load

B. xíngshǐ zhuàngtài
行驶状态
driving state

C. qìhòu tiáojiàn
气候条件
climatic condition

五、小知识　xiǎozhīshi　Tips

新能源汽车的经典广告词大全
Xīnnéngyuán qìchē de jīngdiǎn guǎnggào cí dàquán

1. 驾驭风的感觉，体验美的精致。
   Jiàyù fēng de gǎnjué, tǐyàn měi de jīngzhì.

2. 健康自行，低碳出行。
   Jiànkāng zìxíng, dītàn chūxíng.

3. 放心出行，安心合锂。
   Fàngxīn chūxíng, ānxīn hélǐ.

4. 环保又节能，世界任我行。
   Huánbǎo yòu jiénéng, shìjiè rèn wǒ xíng.

5. 轻松出行，让生活动起来！
   Qīngsōng chūxíng, ràng shēnghuó dòng qǐlái!

Classic Advertisements of New Energy Vehicles

1. Feel the wind and experience the delicacy of beauty.
2. Low-carbon travel, healthy lifestyle.
3. Travel with relaxation and peace.
4. Eco-friendly and energy saving, travel around the world freely.
5. Travel with ease and make life alive!

补充专业词语　bǔchōng zhuānyè cíyǔ　Supplementary Specialized Vocabulary　🎧 10-07

1.	电池衰减	diànchí shuāijiǎn	phr.	battery attenuation
2.	续航里程	xùháng lǐchéng	phr.	range
3.	签约交车	qiānyuē jiāo chē	phr.	contract signing and delivery of vehicles
4.	试乘试驾	shì chéng shì jià	phr.	test drive
5.	产品推荐	chǎnpǐn tuījiàn	phr.	product recommendation
6.	促销活动	cùxiāo huódòng	phr.	sales promotion
7.	汽车载重	qìchē zàizhòng	phr.	auto load
8.	行驶状态	xíngshǐ zhuàngtài	phr.	driving state

第二部分　Part 2

汉字 Chinese Characters

一、汉字知识　Hànzì zhīshi　Knowledge about Chinese Characters

1. 汉字的笔画（总表）Strokes of Chinese characters (general table)

一	丨	丿	丶	、	ㄱ	ㄴ
ㄥ	一	亅	丿	ㄴ	㇀	㇂
乙	ㄑ	乀	㇄	亅	乙	ㄋ
ㄋ	ㄣ	㇌	㇗	㇋	㇅	㇉

2. 汉字的笔顺（总表）Stroke orders of Chinese characters (general table)

笔顺规则 Rules of stroke orders	例字 Examples
先横后竖	十
先撇后捺	人、八
先上后下	三
先左后右	人
先中间后两边	小
先外边后里边	问
先外后里再封口	国、日

3. 汉字的结构（总表）Structures of Chinese characters (general table)

类型 Structure types	结构图示 Illustrations	例字 Examples
独体结构	□	生、不
品字形结构	⊞	品
上下结构	⊟ ⊟	爸、学
上中下结构	☰	意
左右结构	⊟	银、饭
左中右结构	⫼	班、微
全包围结构	▢	国
半包围结构	▢ ▢ ▢ ▢ ▢	医、边、问、唐、凶

128

二、汉字认读与写 Hànzì rèndú yǔ shūxiě The Recognition and Writing of Chinese Characters

认读下列词语，并试着读写构成词语的汉字。
Recognize the following words, and try to read and write the Chinese characters forming these words.

车型　　配置　　优惠　　预算

车			型			配			置		
优			惠			预			算		

第三部分　Part 3　日常用语 Daily Expressions

❶ 谢谢你的礼物，我很喜欢。Xièxie nǐ de lǐwù, wǒ hěn xǐhuan. Thanks for your gift. I like it very much.

❷ 谢谢您的邀请，我一定去。Xièxie nín de yāoqǐng, wǒ yídìng qù. Thanks for your invitation. I will go for sure.

❸ 我该走了，再见。Wǒ gāi zǒu le, zàijiàn. I've got to go. Bye.

第四部分　Part 4　单元实训 Unit Practical Training

模拟推荐电动汽车
Simulated Recommendation of Electric Vehicles

实训目的 Training purpose

通过实训，实训人员能够使用对应电动汽车充电、安全、电池衰减、续航里程、价格等问题的语言技能进行应对，并能分析问题产生的原因。

Through the practical training, the trainees are able to handle charging, safety, battery attenuation, range, price and other problems of electric vehicles with corresponding language skills, and analyze the causes of these problems.

实训组织 Training organization

每组 4 人

four trainees in each group

实训步骤 Training steps

❶ 模拟客户和销售员之间针对充电、安全、电池衰减、续航里程、价格等问题的问答对话。
Simulate the Q&A between customers and salespersons regarding charging, safety, battery attenuation, range, price and other problems.

❷ 学员分组，4人/组。
Divide the trainees into groups of 4.

❸ 学员根据图示自选车型，自编话术。
The trainees choose vehicle models according to the diagrams, and make up their own words.

❹ 小组模拟演练。
Each group conducts simulation exercises.

❺ 学员互评。
The trainees carry out peer assessment.

❻ 教师总结评价，实训结束。
The teacher summarizes and evaluates, and the training ends.

第五部分　Part 5　单元小结　Unit Summary

普通词语　General Vocabulary

cíyǔ
词语　Vocabulary

1.	欢迎光临	huānyíng guānglín	phr.	welcome
2.	店	diàn	n.	store
3.	这么	zhème	pron.	such
4.	天	tiān	n.	weather
5.	辛苦	xīnkǔ	v.	go through hardships
6.	亲自	qīnzì	adv.	in person
7.	过来	guòlái	v.	come over
8.	先	xiān	adv.	first
9.	这边	zhè biān	phr.	here, this side
10.	休息	xiūxi	v.	have a rest
11.	喝	hē	v.	drink
12.	咖啡	kāfēi	n.	coffee
13.	茶	chá	n.	tea
14.	名片	míngpiàn	n.	business card
15.	相比	xiàng bǐ	phr.	compare with each other
16.	强	qiáng	adj.	superior
17.	简易	jiǎnyì	adj.	easy
18.	较低	jiào dī	phr.	relatively low

词语 Vocabulary

19.	完全	wánquán	adv.	completely, totally
20.	取得	qǔdé	v.	gain
21.	兼顾	jiāngù	v.	give consideration to two or more things
22.	无论如何	wúlùn rúhé	phr.	anyway
23.	价格	jiàgé	n.	price
24.	固然	gùrán	conj.	no doubt
25.	选	xuǎn	v.	choose
26.	确定	quèdìng	v.	confirm
27.	详细	xiángxì	adj.	detailed
28.	谈	tán	v.	talk

专业词语　Specialized Vocabulary

1.	专属	zhuānshǔ	adj.	exclusive
2.	销售顾问	xiāoshòu gùwèn	phr.	sales consultant
3.	充电方便	chōngdiàn fāngbiàn	phr.	be easy to charge
4.	稳定性	wěndìngxìng	n.	stability
5.	智能化	zhìnénghuà	v.	be intelligent
6.	补贴	bǔtiē	n.	subsidy
7.	保养	bǎoyǎng	v.	maintain, keep in good repair
8.	外壳	wàiké	n.	outer casing, shell
9.	汽车标准	qìchē biāozhǔn	phr.	automotive standards
10.	制造	zhìzào	v.	manufacture
11.	配	pèi	v.	equip
12.	安全气囊	ānquán qìnáng	phr.	airbag
13.	防撞钢梁	fáng zhuàng gāngliáng	phr.	anti-collision beam
14.	安全配置	ānquán pèizhì	phr.	safety configuration
15.	安全性能	ānquán xìngnéng	phr.	safety performance
16.	优惠幅度	yōuhuì fúdù	phr.	preferential margin

17.	超出预算	chāochū yùsuàn	phr.	beyond the budget
18.	车型	chēxíng	n.	vehicle model
19.	配置	pèizhì	n.	configuration

补充专业词语　Supplementary Specialized Vocabulary

词语 cíyǔ Vocabulary

1.	电池衰减	diànchí shuāijiǎn	phr.	battery attenuation
2.	续航里程	xùháng lǐchéng	phr.	range
3.	签约交车	qiānyuē jiāo chē	phr.	contract signing and delivery of vehicles
4.	试乘试驾	shì chéng shì jià	phr.	test drive
5.	产品推荐	chǎnpǐn tuījiàn	phr.	product recommendation
6.	促销活动	cùxiāo huódòng	phr.	sales promotion
7.	汽车载重	qìchē zàizhòng	phr.	auto load
8.	行驶状态	xíngshǐ zhuàngtài	phr.	driving state

句子 jùzi Sentences

1. 它充电方便，稳定性强，智能化高，操作简易，买车有补贴，并且使用和保养成本都较低。
2. 新能源汽车销售需要做产品推荐，还要试乘试驾，还要做充电方面的指导，要处理消费者提出的异议，比如价格问题，最后签约后交车。
3. 电动汽车销售方法包括要扩大宣传，多办车展，采用降价促销的活动，讲清楚电动汽车的优势和功能，并扩大销售店面，启动线上销售渠道。

附录 Appendixes

词汇总表 Vocabulary

序号	生词	拼音	词性	词义	普通G 专业S	所属 单元
1	啊	a	part.	used at the end of an exclamation for emphasis	G	4A
2	安全配置	ānquán pèizhì	phr.	safety configuration	S	10B
3	安全气囊	ānquán qìnáng	phr.	airbag	S	10B
4	安全性能	ānquán xìngnéng	phr.	safety performance	S	10B
5	按	àn	v.	press	G	3A
6	按照	ànzhào	prep.	according to	G	6A
7	保养	bǎoyǎng	v.	maintain, keep in good repair	S	10A
8	保证	bǎozhèng	v.	ensure, gurantee	G	9A
9	被	bèi	part.	used in a passive sentence to introduce the agent/doer	G	2A
10	比较	bǐjiào	adv.	relatively	G	7A
11	避免	bìmiǎn	v.	avoid	G	5B
12	变化	biànhuà	v.	change	G	9A
13	变速箱	biànsùxiāng	n.	gearbox	S	1
14	表笔	biǎobǐ	n.	probe	S	3A
15	表示	biǎoshì	v.	represent, mean	G	6B
16	表现	biǎoxiàn	n.	performance, behaviour	G	8B
17	并	bìng	adv.	used before a negative for emphasis, usually as a retort	G	6A
18	并联	bìnglián	v.	make a parallel connection	S	6A
19	补偿	bǔcháng	v.	compensate	S	9A
20	补贴	bǔtiē	n.	subsidy	S	10A
21	布局	bùjú	v.	make overall arrangements, lay out	G	6A
22	才	cái	adv.	used to indicate that sth. happens only on certain conditions	G	8B
23	采暖	cǎinuǎn	v.	heat	S	4A
24	采暖系统	cǎinuǎn xìtǒng	phr.	heating system	S	4B
25	踩	cǎi	v.	step on	G	9A
26	操作	cāozuò	v.	operate	S	8B
27	测功机	cègōngjī	n.	dynamometer	S	9
28	茶	chá	n.	tea	G	10A

133

（续表）

序号	生词	拼音	词性	词义	普通G 专业S	所属单元
29	拆解	chāijiě	v.	disassemble	S	2A
30	拆装	chāi zhuāng	phr.	disassemble and assemble	S	8B
31	产品推荐	chǎnpǐn tuījiàn	phr.	product recommendation	S	10
32	常闭继电器	chángbì jìdiànqì	phr.	normally closed relay	S	6B
33	常开继电器	chángkāi jìdiànqì	phr.	normally open relay	S	6B
34	超出预算	chāochū yùsuàn	phr.	beyond the budget	S	10B
35	车灯关闭	chēdēng guānbì	phr.	switch off the car lights	S	6
36	车辆	chēliàng	n.	vehicle	G	1A
37	车轮	chēlún	n.	wheel	G	1A
38	车厢	chēxiāng	n.	compartment, cabin	S	4A
39	车型	chēxíng	n.	vehicle model	S	10B
40	车载充电器	chēzài chōngdiànqì	phr.	on-board charger	S	2A
41	车载电源	chēzài diànyuán	phr.	on-board power supply	S	1A
42	称	chēng	v.	call, name	G	2A
43	成本	chéngběn	n.	cost	G	7A
44	乘车人员	chéng chē rényuán	phr.	passenger	G	4A
45	程度	chéngdù	n.	degree, level	G	4A
46	充电枪	chōngdiànqiāng	n.	charging gun	S	1B
47	充电方便	chōngdiàn fāngbiàn	phr.	be easy to charge	S	10A
48	充电口	chōngdiànkǒu	n.	charging port	S	1B
49	充电桩	chōngdiànzhuāng	n.	charging station	S	1B
50	充放电	chōng-fàngdiàn	v.	charge and discharge	S	5
51	充满电	chōngmǎn diàn	phr.	fully charged	S	8B
52	出现	chūxiàn	v.	occur	G	8B
53	储液罐	chǔyèguàn	n.	liquid storage tank	S	4B
54	传感器	chuángǎnqì	n.	sensor	S	5A
55	串联电池	chuànlián diànchí	phr.	series battery	S	5
56	纯	chún	adj.	pure	G	1A
57	促销活动	cùxiāo huódòng	phr.	sales promotion	S	10
58	DC/DC 转换器	DC/DC zhuǎnhuànqì	phr.	DC-to-DC converter	S	3
59	达到	dádào	v.	reach	G	9B
60	大于	dàyú	v.	be greater/larger than	G	3B
61	代表	dàibiǎo	v.	represent	G	6A

134

（续表）

序号	生词	拼音	词性	词义	普通G 专业S	所属 单元
62	单线制	dānxiànzhì	n.	single-wire system	S	6A
63	导线	dǎoxiàn	n.	lead	S	6A
64	等	děng	part.	etc., and so on	G	2B
65	低	dī	adj.	low	G	1A
66	低压电池	dīyā diànchí	phr.	low-voltage battery	S	1B
67	低压控制线束	dīyā kòngzhì xiànshù	phr.	low-voltage control wiring harness	S	7A
68	低压配电系统	dīyā pèidiàn xìtǒng	phr.	low-voltage power distribution system	S	1A
69	低压通信线	dīyā tōngxìnxiàn	phr.	low-voltage communication line	S	1
70	底板线束	dǐbǎn xiànshù	phr.	chassis base wiring harness	S	6B
71	典型	diǎnxíng	adj.	typical	G	5A
72	点火开关	diǎnhuǒ kāiguān	phr.	ignition switch	S	6
73	电池衰减	diànchí shuāijiǎn	phr.	battery attenuation	S	10
74	电池智能传感器	diànchí zhìnéng chuángǎnqì	phr.	battery smart sensor	S	5A
75	电磁阀	diàncífá	n.	solenoid valve	S	6B
76	电动冷却液泵	diàndòng lěngquèyèbèng	phr.	electric coolant pump	S	4B
77	电机控制器	diànjī kòngzhìqì	phr.	motor controller	S	2A
78	电力	diànlì	n.	electric power	S	1A
79	电量不足	diànliàng bùzú	phr.	low battery	S	8B
80	电流	diànliú	n.	electric current	S	2
81	电流传感器	diànliú chuángǎnqì	phr.	current sensor	S	5A
82	电路	diànlù	n.	circuit	S	2B
83	电路图	diànlùtú	n.	circuit diagram	S	6A
84	电气元件	diànqì yuánjiàn	phr.	electrical component	S	6A
85	店	diàn	n.	store	G	10A
86	顶棚线束	dǐngpéng xiànshù	phr.	roof wiring harness	S	6B
87	定子	dìngzǐ	n.	stator	S	5B
88	动力电池系统	dònglì diànchí xìtǒng	phr.	power battery system	S	1A
89	动力电机系统	dònglì diànjī xìtǒng	phr.	power motor system	S	1A
90	动力线束	dònglì xiànshù	phr.	power wiring harness	S	6B
91	动力蓄电池组	dònglì xùdiànchízǔ	phr.	power storage battery pack	S	4
92	短接	duǎnjiē	v.	short-circuit	S	3A
93	断电	duàndiàn	phr.	power off	S	3A

（续表）

序号	生词	拼音	词性	词义	普通G 专业S	所属单元
94	对应	duìyìng	v.	match	G	6A
95	发动机舱线束	fādòng jīcāng xiànshù	phr.	engine compartment wiring harness	S	6B
96	发生	fāshēng	v.	happen	G	8B
97	反方向	fǎn fāngxiàng	phr.	reverse direction	S	9B
98	方面	fāngmiàn	n.	aspect	G	7A
99	防撞钢梁	fáng zhuàng gāngliáng	phr.	anti-collision beam	S	10B
100	分	fēn	v.	divide	G	4B
102	分别	fēnbié	adv.	respectively	G	4B
103	分布均匀	fēnbù jūnyún	phr.	uniform distribution	G	9A
104	分开	fēnkāi	v.	separate	G	3A
105	负担	fùdān	n.	burden	S	4
106	负极	fùjí	n.	negative pole	S	3
107	刚才	gāngcái	n.	the time just past	G	5B
108	高低压管路	gāo-dīyā guǎnlù	phr.	high-pressure and low-pressure pipelines	S	4B
109	高压电控系统	gāoyā diànkòng xìtǒng	phr.	high-voltage electronic control system	S	1A
110	高压电控总成	gāoyā diànkòng zǒngchéng	phr.	high-voltage electronic control assembly	S	1B
111	高压动力线	gāoyā dònglìxiàn	phr.	high-voltage power line	S	1
112	高压控制盒	gāoyā kòngzhìhé	phr.	high-voltage control box	S	2A
113	高压线束	gāoyā xiànshù	phr.	high-voltage wiring harness	S	7A
114	各	gè	pron.	each	G	4B
115	更	gèng	adv.	more	G	7B
116	工作原理	gōngzuò yuánlǐ	phr.	working principle	S	8A
117	公式	gōngshì	n.	formula	G	9A
118	供	gōng	v.	provide	S	1B
119	鼓风机	gǔfēngjī	n.	blower	S	4B
120	固然	gùrán	conj.	no doubt	G	10B
121	故障	gùzhàng	n.	breakdown, malfunction	S	8B
122	关联	guānlián	v.	be linked	S	6A
123	观察	guānchá	v.	observe	G	3A
124	管理	guǎnlǐ	v.	manage	G	1B
125	过	guò	adv.	excessively, too	G	5B
126	过来	guòlái	v.	come over	G	10A

（续表）

序号	生词	拼音	词性	词义	普通G 专业S	所属单元
127	行车	xíngchē	v.	drive	S	4A
128	行驶状态	xíngshǐ zhuàngtài	phr.	driving state	S	10
129	耗电量	hàodiànliàng	n.	power consumption	S	4
130	喝	hē	v.	drink	G	10A
131	合格	hégé	adj.	qualified	S	2
132	合理	hélǐ	adj.	reasonable	G	6A
133	合适	héshì	adj.	appropriate, suitable	G	2B
134	黑色	hēisè	n.	black	G	6A
135	后端盖	hòuduāngài	n.	rear end cover	S	5B
136	化学能	huàxuénéng	n.	chemical energy	S	8A
137	欢迎光临	huānyíng guānglín	phr.	welcome	G	10A
138	环境	huánjìng	n.	environment	G	4A
139	会	huì	aux.	be likely to	G	8B
140	机舱	jīcāng	n.	engine room	S	2A
141	机电维修工	jīdiàn wéixiūgōng	phr.	mechanical and electrical maintenance technician	S	5A
142	机械	jīxiè	n.	machinery	S	2
143	集成	jíchéng	v.	integrate	S	2A
144	几	jǐ	pron.	several	G	5B
145	计算	jìsuàn	v.	calculate	G	9A
146	记录	jìlù	v.	record	G	9A
147	记住	jìzhù	v.	remember	G	2A
148	技术总监	jìshù zǒngjiān	phr.	technical director	S	5A
149	加热器	jiārèqì	n.	heater	S	4B
150	加速	jiāsù	v.	accelerate	S	9B
151	加速踏板	jiāsù tàbǎn	n.	accelerator pedal	S	9A
152	加载	jiāzài	v.	load	S	9A
153	家用	jiāyòng	adj.	for household use, domestic	G	7A
154	价格	jiàgé	n.	price	G	10B
155	兼顾	jiāngù	v.	give consideration to two or more things	G	10B
156	检测	jiǎncè	v.	detect	S	2B
157	检查	jiǎnchá	v.	check	G	3A
158	简写	jiǎnxiě	n.	abbreviation	G	6A

（续表）

序号	生词	拼音	词性	词义	普通G 专业S	所属 单元
159	简易	jiǎnyì	adj.	easy	G	10A
160	将	jiāng	prep.	used to introduce the object before the verb	G	3A
161	降低	jiàngdī	v.	reduce	G	4A
162	交流	jiāoliú	n.	AC, alternating current	S	2B
163	交流充电	jiāoliú chōngdiàn	phr.	AC charging	S	7A
164	交流充电桩	jiāoliú chōngdiànzhuāng	phr.	AC charging station	S	7A
165	交流电源	jiāoliú diànyuán	phr.	AC power supply	S	7A
166	焦煳味	jiāohúwèi	n.	burnt smell	G	8B
167	较低	jiào dī	phr.	relatively low	G	10A
168	接地	jiēdì	v.	ground	S	6A
169	接下来	jiē xiàlái	phr.	next	G	3A
170	结构单元	jiégòu dānyuán	phr.	structural unit	S	2
171	进行	jìnxíng	v.	proceed	G	2B
172	净化	jìnghuà	v.	purify	S	4A
173	绝缘	juéyuán	v.	insulate	S	8
174	绝缘电阻	juéyuán diànzǔ	phr.	insulation resistance	S	3B
175	绝缘垫	juéyuándiàn	n.	insulating mat	S	3B
176	绝缘性能	juéyuán xìngnéng	phr.	insulation performance	S	3B
177	咖啡	kāfēi	n.	coffee	G	10A
178	开关	kāiguān	n.	switch	S	3A
179	可能	kěnéng	v.	maybe, perhaps	G	5A
180	空气	kōngqì	n.	air	G	4A
181	空气净化系统	kōngqì jìnghuà xìtǒng	phr.	air purification system	S	4B
182	空调	kōngtiáo	n.	air conditioning, air conditioner	G	4A
183	空调系统	kōngtiáo xìtǒng	phr.	air conditioning system	S	4A
184	空调压缩机	kōngtiáo yāsuōjī	phr.	air conditioning compressor	S	3
185	控制	kòngzhì	v.	control	G	2B
186	快充插座	kuàichōng chāzuò	phr.	quick charging socket	S	7B
187	快速	kuàisù	adj.	fast	G	7B
188	款	kuǎn	m.	kind	G	6A
189	冷凝器	lěngníngqì	n.	condenser	S	4B
190	里程	lǐchéng	n.	mileage	S	9A

（续表）

序号	生词	拼音	词性	词义	普通 G 专业 S	所属单元
191	零	líng	num.	zero	G	1A
192	流程	liúchéng	n.	process, procedure	S	3
193	漏电	lòudiàn	v.	(of electricity) leak	S	2B
194	漏液	lòu yè	phr.	liquid leakage	S	8B
195	轮胎气压	lúntāi qìyā	phr.	tire pressure	S	9
196	慢	màn	adj.	slow	G	7A
197	慢速	mànsù	adj.	low speed	G	7A
198	没错	méi cuò	phr.	correct, right	G	7B
199	门线束	mén xiànshù	phr.	door wiring harness	S	6B
200	名片	míngpiàn	n.	business card	G	10A
201	呢	ne	part.	used at the end of a question	G	1B
202	内部	nèibù	n.	inside	G	5B
203	扭曲	niǔqū	v.	distort	S	8B
204	排放	páifàng	v.	emit	S	1A
205	旁边	pángbiān	n.	side	G	6A
206	跑道	pǎodào	n.	track	S	9
207	配	pèi	v.	equip	S	10B
208	配置	pèizhì	n.	configuration	S	10B
209	膨胀阀	péngzhàngfá	n.	expansion valve	S	4B
210	疲劳	píláo	adj.	tired	G	4A
211	平均	píngjūn	v.	average	G	9A
212	平均值	píngjūn zhí	phr.	average value	S	9B
213	起始位置	qǐshǐ wèizhì	phr.	starting position	G	9B
214	汽车标准	qìchē biāozhǔn	phr.	automotive standards	S	10B
215	汽车载重	qìchē zàizhòng	phr.	auto load	S	10
216	签约交车	qiānyuē jiāo chē	phr.	contract signing and delivery of vehicles	S	10
217	前	qián	n.	front	G	2A
218	强	qiáng	adj.	superior	G	10A
219	亲自	qīnzì	adv.	in person	G	10A
220	清晰	qīngxī	adj.	clear	G	6A
221	情况	qíngkuàng	n.	circumstance	G	8B
222	驱动电机	qūdòng diànjī	phr.	driving motor	S	1B
223	取得	qǔdé	v.	gain	G	10B

（续表）

序号	生词	拼音	词性	词义	普通G 专业S	所属单元
224	确定	quèdìng	v.	confirm	G	10B
225	然后	ránhòu	conj.	then	G	9A
226	热	rè	adj.	hot	G	4A
227	仍然	réngrán	adv.	still	G	8B
228	如何	rúhé	pron.	how	G	1B
229	若	ruò	conj.	if	G	9A
230	SOC检测	SOC jiǎncè	phr.	SOC test	S	8
231	设备	shèbèi	n.	equipment	S	6A
232	设定	shèdìng	v.	set	S	4
233	甚至	shènzhì	conj.	even	G	8B
234	生产	shēngchǎn	v.	manufacture	S	2
235	湿度	shīdù	n.	humidity	S	9
236	实际	shíjì	adj.	actual	G	6A
237	实际上	shíjì shang	phr.	in fact, actually	G	8A
238	试	shì	v.	try	G	7B
239	试乘试驾	shì chéng shì jià	phr.	test drive	S	10
240	试验	shìyàn	n.	test	S	9A
241	是否	shìfǒu	adv.	whether	G	3A
242	寿命	shòumìng	n.	life, lifespan	S	2
243	舒适	shūshì	adj.	comfortable	G	4A
244	输出	shūchū	v.	output	S	2B
245	输入	shūrù	v.	input	S	2B
246	数量	shùliàng	n.	quantity	G	7A
247	数值	shùzhí	n.	value	S	3A
248	说明	shuōmíng	v.	indicate, show	G	3A
249	四合一	sì hé yī	phr.	four-in-one	S	2A
250	损坏	sǔnhuài	v.	damage	G	5B
251	缩写	suōxiě	n.	abbreviation	G	6B
252	台	tái	m.	used for certain machines, apparatuses, etc.	G	5A
253	太	tài	adv.	too	G	7B
254	谈	tán	v.	talk	G	10B
255	特点	tèdiǎn	n.	characteristic	G	1A

（续表）

序号	生词	拼音	词性	词义	普通 G 专业 S	所属单元
256	提高	tígāo	v.	improve	G	4A
257	提供	tígōng	v.	provide	G	8A
258	天	tiān	n.	weather	G	10A
259	天气	tiānqì	n.	weather	G	4A
260	条件	tiáojiàn	n.	condition	G	7A
261	通常	tōngcháng	adv.	usually	G	1B
262	通电	tōngdiàn	phr.	power on	S	3A
263	通风	tōngfēng	v.	ventilate	S	4A
264	通风系统	tōngfēng xìtǒng	phr.	ventilation system	S	4B
265	通过	tōngguò	prep.	through	G	9A
266	图形	túxíng	n.	graph, figure	G	6B
267	外观	wàiguān	n.	appearance	S	8B
268	外壳	wàiké	n.	outer casing, shell	S	10B
269	完全	wánquán	adv.	completely, totally	G	10B
270	为	wéi	v.	act as	G	1A
271	为什么	wèi shénme	phr.	why	G	7A
272	位于	wèiyú	v.	locate	G	1B
273	位置	wèizhì	n.	position, location	G	5A
274	温差	wēnchā	n.	temperature difference	S	4
275	温度	wēndù	n.	temperature	G	5A
276	温度传感器	wēndù chuángǎnqì	phr.	temperature sensor	S	5A
277	稳定性	wěndìngxìng	n.	stability	SS	10A
278	问题	wèntí	n.	problem	G	5A
279	无论如何	wúlùn rúhé	phr.	anyway	G	10B
280	先	xiān	adv.	first	G	10A
281	显示	xiǎnshì	v.	show, display	S	8B
282	相比	xiàng bǐ	phr.	compare with each other	G	10A
283	详细	xiángxì	adj.	detailed	G	10B
284	项	xiàng	m.	item	G	3A
285	销售顾问	xiāoshòu gùwèn	phr.	sales consultant	S	10A
286	小负载保险丝	xiǎo fùzài bǎoxiǎnsī	phr.	small load fuse	S	6B
287	辛苦	xīnkǔ	v.	go through hardships	G	10A
288	新能源	xīnnéngyuán	n.	new energy	S	8A

（续表）

序号	生词	拼音	词性	词义	普通G 专业S	所属单元
289	性能	xìngnéng	n.	performance	S	9B
290	休息	xiūxi	v.	have a rest	G	10A
291	续航里程	xùháng lǐchéng	phr.	range	S	10
292	旋变传感器	xuánbiàn chuángǎnqì	phr.	resolver	S	5A
293	选	xuǎn	v.	choose	G	10B
294	选择	xuǎnzé	v.	select	G	3A
295	压缩机	yāsuōjī	n.	compressor	S	4B
296	要求	yāoqiú	n.	requirement	G	7B
297	依据	yījù	prep.	according to	G	6A
298	依靠	yīkào	v.	depend on, rely on	G	1A
299	仪表线束	yíbiǎo xiànshù	phr.	instrument panel wiring harness	S	6B
300	一会儿	yíhuìr	q.	soon	G	4A
301	以后	yǐhòu	n.	afterwards	G	9B
302	以及	yǐjí	conj.	and	G	4B
303	一般	yìbān	adv.	generally	G	2A
304	意思	yìsi	n.	meaning	G	6B
305	因为	yīnwèi	conj.	because, due to	G	7A
306	引擎盖	yǐnqínggài	n.	hood	S	1B
307	优惠幅度	yōuhuì fúdù	phr.	preferential margin	S	10B
308	优势	yōushì	n.	advantage	G	7A
309	又	yòu	adv.	also	G	2A
310	原理	yuánlǐ	n.	principle	G	6A
311	允许	yǔnxǔ	v.	allow	G	2A
312	载荷	zàihè	n.	load	S	9A
313	造成	zàochéng	v.	cause	G	5B
314	噪声	zàoshēng	n.	noise	G	1A
315	展示	zhǎnshì	v.	display, demonstrate	G	6A
316	兆欧表	zhào'ōubiǎo	n.	megger	S	3A
317	这边	zhè biān	phr.	here, this side	G	10A
318	这么	zhème	pron.	such	G	10A
319	这些	zhèxiē	pron.	these	G	6B
320	这样	zhèyàng	pron.	such	G	9B
321	真	zhēn	adv.	truly	G	4A

（续表）

序号	生词	拼音	词性	词义	普通G 专业S	所属单元
322	蒸发器	zhēngfāqì	n.	evaporator	S	4B
323	整车控制器	zhěngchē kòngzhìqì	phr.	vehicle control unit (VCU)	S	7A
324	整个	zhěnggè	adj.	whole	G	6A
325	正常	zhèngcháng	adj.	normal	G	3A
326	正极	zhèngjí	n.	positive pole	S	3
327	之后	zhīhòu	n.	later	G	9A
328	只有	zhǐyǒu	conj.	only	G	8B
329	直流	zhíliú	n.	DC, direct current	S	2B
330	直流变压器	zhíliú biànyāqì	phr.	DC-to-DC converter	S	2A
331	直流充电	Zhíliú chōngdiàn	phr.	charging	S	7B
332	直流充电桩	zhíliú chōngdiànzhuāng	phr.	DC charging station	S	7B
333	指	zhǐ	v.	refer to	G	1A
334	制冷	zhìlěng	v.	refrigerate cool	S	4A
335	制冷系统	zhìlěng xìtǒng	phr.	refrigeration system	S	4B
336	制造	zhìzào	v.	manufacture	S	10B
337	质量	zhìliàng	n.	quality	S	9A
338	智能化	zhìnénghuà	v.	be intelligent	S	10A
339	种	zhǒng	m.	type, kind	G	8A
340	专属	zhuānshǔ	adj.	exclusive	S	10A
341	转化	zhuǎnhuà	v.	convert	G	2B
342	转动	zhuàndòng	v.	rotate	S	1B
343	转子	zhuànzǐ	n.	rotor	S	5B
344	装置	zhuāngzhì	n.	device	S	4A
345	字母	zìmǔ	n.	letter	G	6B
346	阻值	zǔzhí	n.	resistance value	S	3B
347	组件	zǔjiàn	n.	component	S	5B
348	最高车速	zuì gāo chēsù	phr	maximum speed	S	9A

视频脚本　Video Scripts

第一单元　电动汽车简介

一、热身
电动汽车主要部件包括动力蓄电池、高压电控总成、驱动电机、转向系统、充电口等。

三、视听说
徒弟：师傅，这些电动汽车零部件分别是什么？
师傅：这些零部件分别是：充电口、充电桩、充电枪、低压电池、高压电控总成、驱动电机、动力蓄电池、电池管理系统。

四、学以致用
徒弟：师傅，电动汽车的上电流程是什么？
师傅：低压电池先供电，高压电控总成上电之后，驱动电机转动，驱动车辆行驶。

第二单元　电动汽车高压电控总成

一、热身
比亚迪 e5 电动汽车高压电控总成"四合一"是一个大盒子。它的正面有三个插座，从左往右的作用分别是交流输入、三相交流输出和直流输入。

三、视听说
电动汽车高压电控总成包括车载充电器、DC-DC、电机控制器、高压控制盒四个部分。当汽车没电时，可以使用车载充电器给汽车充电。DC-DC 将直流高压转化为直流低压，供车灯、控制器等低压电器使用。电机控制器控制驱动电机，使车辆可以正常行驶。高压控制盒用来控制高压电流输入和输出，并检测高压电流和漏电情况。

四、学以致用
徒弟：师傅，电动汽车如果没电了应该怎么办？
师傅：当汽车没电时，一般有两种方式可以给汽车充电，分别叫作快充和慢充。快充也就是直流充电，需要专用的直流充电桩，充电速度快，通常 15～2 个小时就可以完成。慢充也叫作交流充电，需要借助车载充电机完成，充电速度慢，通常需要 8～12 个小时才能完成。快充的电流和功率较大，会影响动力蓄电池组寿命。

第三单元　电动汽车绝缘检测

一、热身
徒弟：师傅，电动汽车绝缘检测流程是什么？
师傅：首先进行兆欧表自检，然后检测绝缘垫，最后进行高压部件检测。

三、视听说
徒弟：师傅，如何对高压部件进行绝缘检测？电阻值分别是多少说明绝缘性能良好呢？
师傅：我来给你演示下检测流程，另外你要记住这些数值哦：动力蓄电池是正极 ≥14MΩ，负极 ≥10MΩ；电机控制器和驱动电机是 ≥100MΩ；高压线束和高压熔断器盒是无穷大 ∞；空调压缩机是 ≥5MΩ 或 ≥50MΩ；车载充电机和 DC/DC 转换器是 ≥100MΩ 或 ≥20MΩ；加热器（PTC）是 ≥500MΩ。

四、学以致用

师傅：徒弟，你去把这辆电动汽车绝缘垫检测一下。

徒弟：好的，师傅。

师傅：绝缘垫车前、车后、车左、车右、车中5个点的绝缘电阻值都要大于20MΩ。

徒弟：师傅，经过检测，绝缘垫B点的阻值为5MΩ，A、B、C、E点的阻值均大于20MΩ。

第四单元　空调系统

一、热身

电动汽车的空调系统包括冷凝器、压缩机、加热器、电动冷却液泵等组成部分。它们的作用各不相同。压缩机和冷凝器是制冷系统的重要组成部分，加热器和电动冷却液泵是采暖系统的重要组成部分。

三、视听说

打开空调"A/C"开关，电机驱动压缩机工作，制冷系统开启。

首先，压缩机对制冷剂进行压缩，制冷剂的温度和压力升高。

其次，制冷剂进入冷凝器，将热量传递到车外，制冷剂的温度降低，液化。

然后，制冷剂经过膨胀阀，压力降低。

最后，制冷剂进入蒸发器，吸收车内热量，制冷剂汽化。

如此，制冷剂在空调系统中形成循环，从而达到制冷的目的。

四、学以致用

当空调系统处于采暖模式时，加热器对冷却液进行加热，冷却液温度升高。电动冷却液泵将高温冷却液抽入加热器芯。同时，车外新鲜风和车内循环风在鼓风机的作用下流过加热器芯。外部空气与加热后的空气混合，吹出舒适的暖风。

第五单元　典型传感器

一、热身

旋变传感器、温度传感器和电流传感器都安装在驱动电机上；电池智能传感器安装在电池管理系统中。

三、视听说

旋变传感器检测位置，温度传感器检测温度，电流传感器检测电流，电池智能传感器检测SOC、电压、电流和温度。

四、学以致用

温度传感器安装在驱动电机的后端盖里面，旋变传感器安装在定子上。

第六单元　电路图识读

一、热身

徒弟：师傅，这些图形在电路图中是什么含义？

师傅：这些图形分别表示接地、小负载保险丝、常闭继电器、温度传感器、蓄电池、常开继电器、电磁阀、双绞线、加热器。

三、视听说

徒弟：师傅，这些线束代码是什么意思？

师傅：CA表示发动机舱线束，BV表示动力线束，IP表示仪表线束，SO表示底板线束，DR表示门线束，RF表示顶棚线束。

四、学以致用

　　保险丝在 IG1 和 IP01 的 13 号端子之间，IP01 的 30 号端子和 31 号端子连接的导线是双绞线，IP01 的 16 号端子连接导线接地。

第七单元　充电系统

一、热身

徒弟：师傅，请问电动汽车充电系统有哪些类型呢？
师傅：电动汽车充电系统包括交流慢速充电系统和直流快速充电系统。

三、视听说

　　不同国家充电桩的插头是不一样的，北美采用的是……，欧洲采用的是……，日本采用的是……，中国采用的是……

四、学以致用

1 A：我的电动汽车快没电了，怎么办？我 2 小时后就要去火车站接爷爷奶奶了。
　B：快去给汽车快充一下电吧，来得及。
2 A：您好，我买了一辆电动汽车需要安装充电桩，可是我的小区很小，可以安装吗？
　B：可以的，但是只能选择交流充电桩了，给您安装交流充电桩吧。
3 A：两天后我就要出去自驾游啦，好开心呀。
　B：那你记得提前一天给电动汽车充满电哦。
4 A：你家小区有充电桩吗？我的电动汽车没电了。
　B：有的，我们小区都是直流充电桩，充电非常快。

第八单元　动力蓄电池拆装

一、热身

　　绝缘防护准备包括四步：1 准备绝缘工具。2 准备维修仪表。3 穿戴上绝缘服。4 在地上铺上绝缘垫。

三、视听说

1 准备维修工具及检测仪表。
2 穿戴高压防护装备，在地上铺上绝缘垫。
3 关闭点火开关。
4 断开低压蓄电池的负极。
5 拆除维修开关。
6 举升车辆，检查动力蓄电池底部。
7 拆下动力蓄电池底部。
8 拆动力蓄电池的高压插件。
9 将动力蓄电池举升车推到动力蓄电池正下方。
10 举升电池举升车，与电池底部接触。
11 拆下固定螺栓。
12 缓慢下降动力蓄电池举升车，降到需要的高度后，推出动力蓄电池举升车。

四、学以致用

1 准备维修工具及检测仪表。
2 穿戴高压防护装备。
3 缓慢上升动力蓄电池举升车，推入动力电池。
4 确保动力蓄电池箱体的定位销对准底盘上的定位孔，插上定位拴。
5 接上低压蓄电池的负极端子。

6 接通动力蓄电池高压插件。
7 装上动力蓄电池底板。
8 SOC 检测。

第九单元　电动汽车试验

一、热身
1 选择合适的测试环境，将试验车辆加载到规定质量，保证载荷分布均匀。
2 在直线跑道或者环形跑道上将车辆加速到最高稳定车速，并保证以这个车速持续行驶 1 千米。
3 记录车辆持续行驶的时间 t1，再做一次反方向试验，记录时间 t2。
4 用公式计算车速：速度 =3600/t，t=(t1+t2)/2。

三、视听说
1 将试验车辆加载到试验质量，保证载荷分布均匀。
2 将车辆置于测功机，调整到适合试验车辆的质量。
3 调整测功机，增加一个相当于 4% 坡度的附加载荷。
4 加速试验车辆，达到并能持续行驶 1km 的最高稳定车速，记录时间 t1。
5 再调整测功机，使其增加一个相当于 12% 坡度的附加载荷，重复试验，记录 t2。
6 最后停车检查各部件有无异常现象发生，并详细记录。

四、学以致用
1 试验车辆在完成"30 分钟最高车速"试验之后，将车辆停放 30 分钟。
2 以 30 分钟最高车速的 70% 的速度恢复行驶，直到车速下降到油门踩到底时，车速为"30 分钟最高车速试验中的车速 V30 的 70% 恢复行驶"；或是直到仪表板上的信号装置提示停车。记录行驶里程。
3 然后计算总的行驶里程 = 预热阶段行驶里程 ±V30 试验的行驶里程 + 完全放电时的行驶里程。

第十单元　电动汽车销售

一、热身
徒弟：师傅，请问电动汽车销售和燃油汽车销售有什么不同吗？
师傅：首先因为消费者不太了解，所以需要做产品推荐，还要试乘试驾，还要做充电方面的指导，要处理消费者提出的异议，比如价格问题，最后签约后交车。

三、视听说
徒弟：师傅，电动汽车是一种新的车型，相对而言，很多人都不知道，我们怎样促进销售呢？
师傅：我们一定要扩大宣传，多办车展，采用降价促销的活动，讲清楚电动汽车的优势和功能，并扩大销售店面，启动线上销售渠道。

四、学以致用
客户 1：我在 0 度左右使用比亚迪汉 EV 采暖，第一小时大约 4KW/小时，持续使用大约 2KW/小时，是什么原因呢？
销售员：影响电动汽车续驶里程的因素有很多，你这种情况是因为行驶的时候使用了采暖。
客户 2：为什么我的比亚迪电动汽车充电最多只能充 80%。
销售员：外界环境对充电影响很大，尤其是气温越低，充电效果越差。
客户 3：为什么里程表显示只能开 200 公里了。
销售员：请问车上坐了几个人？
客户 3：今天坐满了 5 个人。
销售员：车载质量太大也会影响续驶里程。

参考答案　Reference Answers

第一单元　电动汽车简介

一、热身

1. ①B　②C　③D　④A　⑤F　⑥E
2.

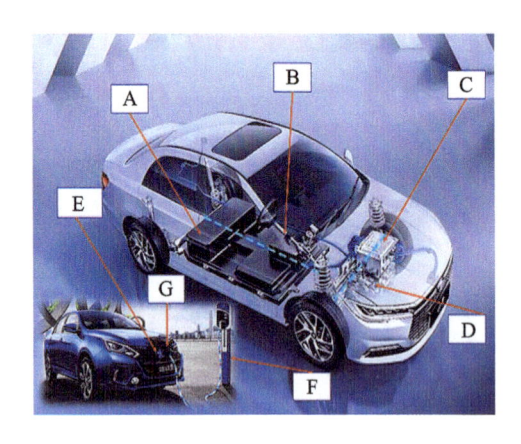

三、视听说

1. B　2. D　3. F　4. A　5. H　6. G　7. E　8. C

四、学以致用

1. C　2. A　3. B

第二单元　电动汽车高压电控总成

一、热身

1. ①B　②C　③A
2. ①B　②D　③A　④C

三、视听说

1. D　2. C　3. A　4. B

四、学以致用

1. B　2. A　3. A

第三单元　电动汽车绝缘检测

一、热身

1. ①A　②C　③B　④D　⑤F　⑥E
2. ①C　②A　③B

三、试听说

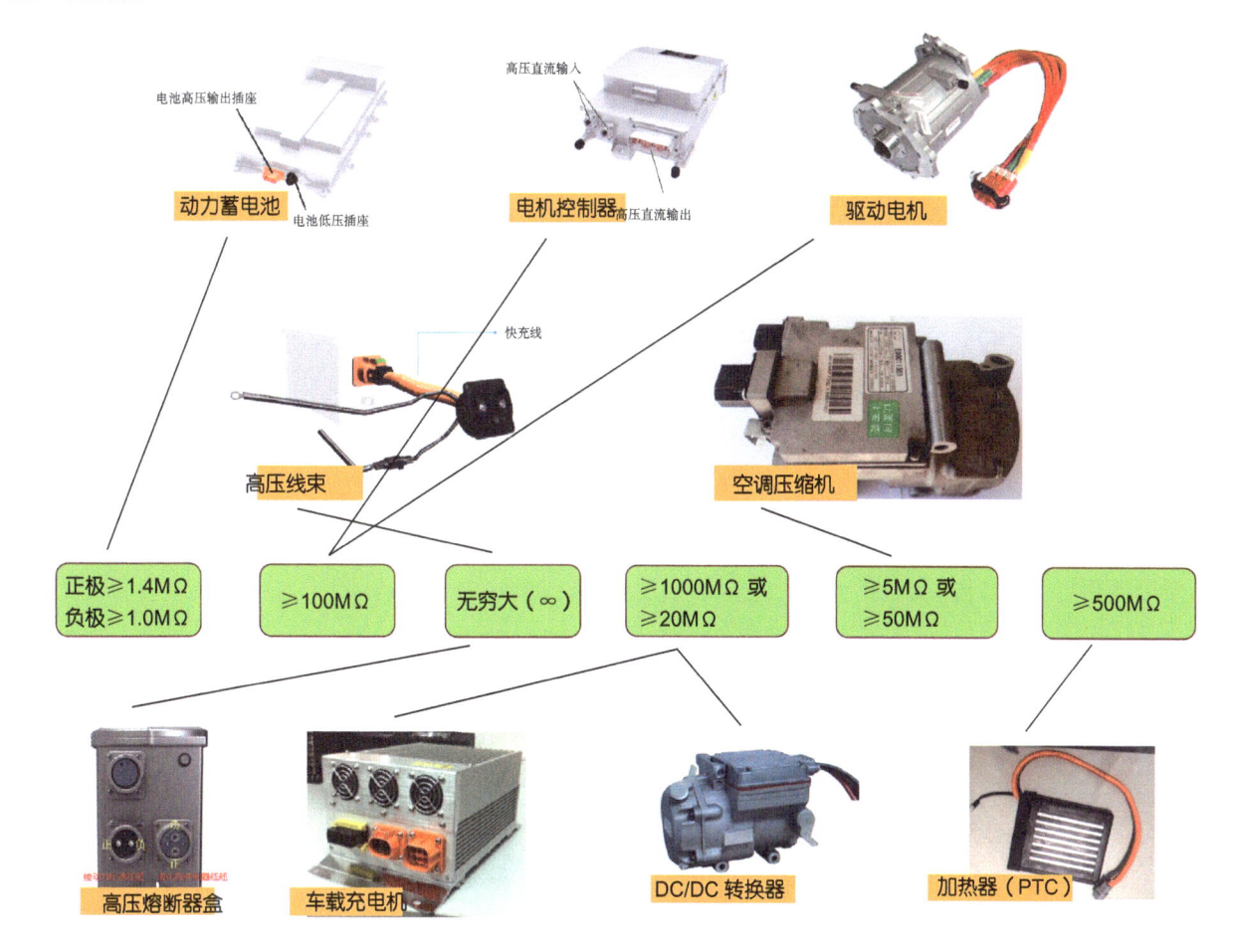

四、学以致用

1. ADCE   2. B

第四单元　空调系统

一、热身

1. ①C   ②D   ③A   ④B
2. ①B   ②A   ③D   ④C

三、视听说

1. C   2. B   3. A

四、学以致用

1. C   2. A   3. B

第五单元　典型传感器

一、热身

1. ①B   ②A   ③D   ④C
2. ①ABD   ②C

三、视听说

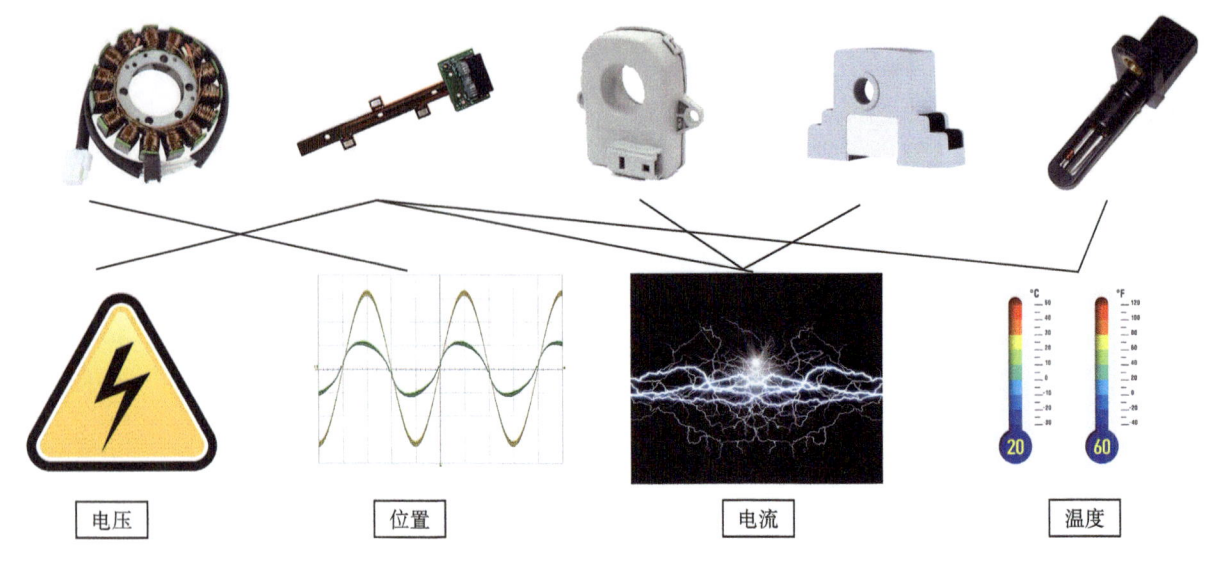

电压	位置	电流	温度

四、学以致用

1. E   2. C

第六单元　电路图识读

一、热身

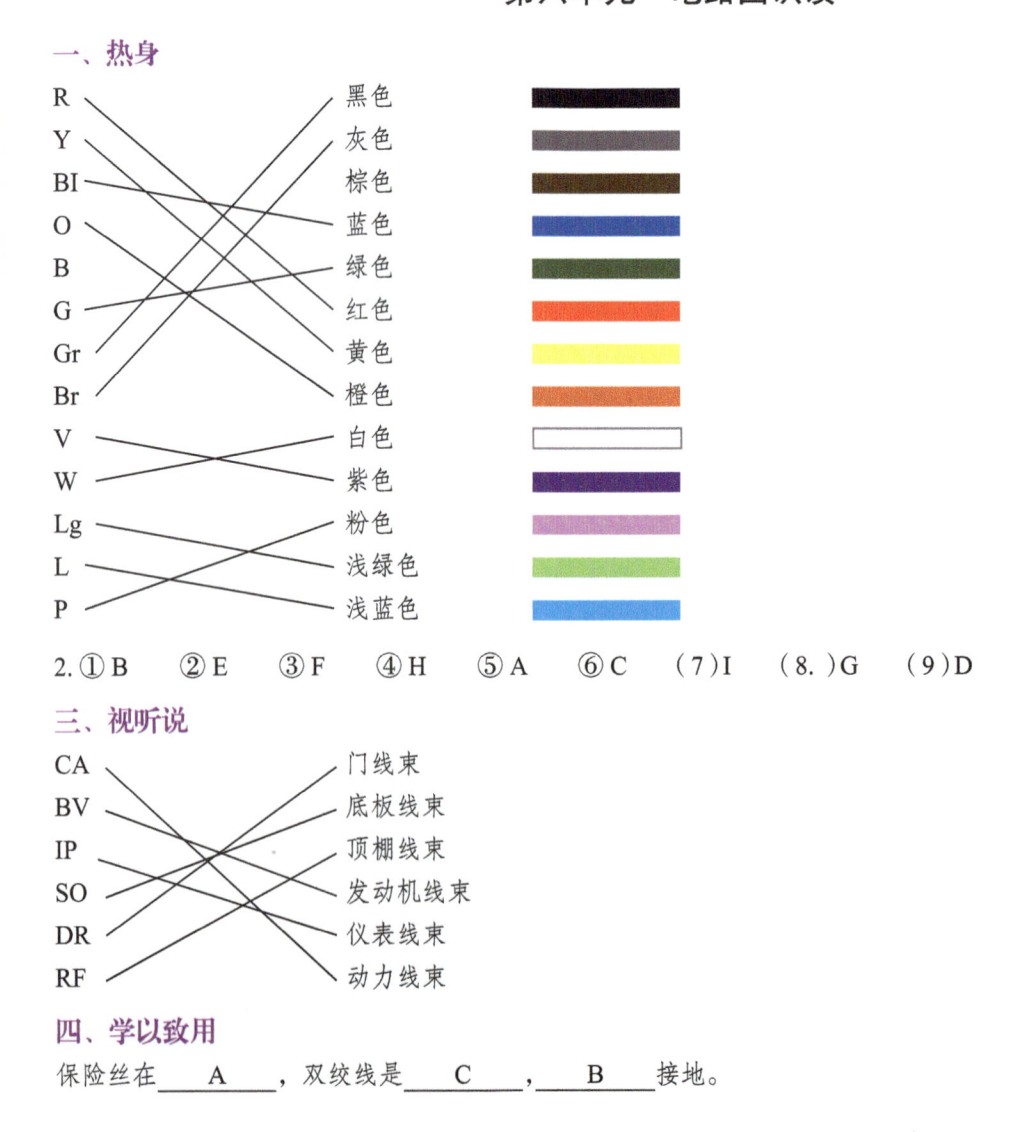

R — 黑色
Y — 灰色
Bl — 棕色
O — 蓝色
B — 绿色
G — 红色
Gr — 黄色
Br — 橙色
V — 白色
W — 紫色
Lg — 粉色
L — 浅绿色
P — 浅蓝色

2. ① B   ② E   ③ F   ④ H   ⑤ A   ⑥ C   （7）I   （8.）G   （9）D

三、视听说

CA — 门线束
BV — 底板线束
IP — 顶棚线束
SO — 发动机线束
DR — 仪表线束
RF — 动力线束

四、学以致用

保险丝在＿＿A＿＿，双绞线是＿＿C＿＿，＿B＿接地。

第七单元　充电系统

一、热身

1. ① A　② C　③ B　④ D　⑤ F　⑥ E
2. ① A　② C

三、试听说

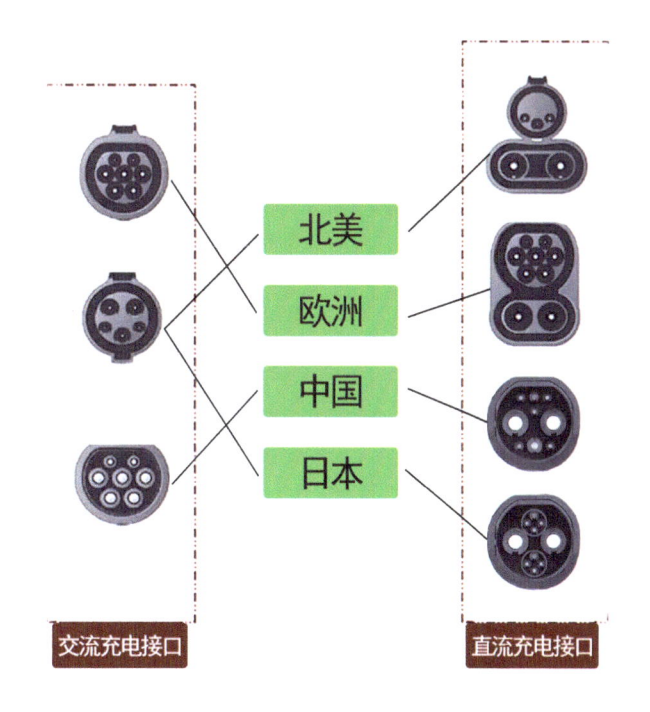

四、学以致用

1. 直流充电：AD　　2. 交流充电：BC

第八单元　动力蓄电池拆装

一、热身

1. ① E　② F　③ D　④ C　⑤ A　⑥ B
2. ① B　② A　③ D　④ C

三、视听说

1. B　2. A　3. D　4. E　5. C

四、学以致用

1. D　2. B　3. E　4. C　5. A

第九单元　电动汽车试验

一、热身

1. ① C　② A　③ B　④ D　⑤ E　⑥ F
2. ① B　② A　③ B　④ C

三、视听说

1. F　2. A　3. C　4. B　5. D　6. E

四、学以致用

1. E　2. A　3. C　4. B　5. D

第十单元　电动汽车销售

一、热身

1. ①C　②D　③B　④A
2. ①D　②C　③A　④B

四、试听说

1. C　2. D　3. A　4. B　5. E

五、学以致用

1. B　2. C　3. A